HOLY $moke!

Whatever Happened to Tithing?

J. Clif Christopher and Herb Mather

DISCIPLESHIP RESOURCES

P.O. BOX 340003 • NASHVILLE, TN 37203-0003

www.discipleshipresources.org

Cover design by Sharon Anderson.

Book design by Joey McNair.

ISBN 0-88177-284-4

Library of Congress Catalog Card No. 99-61197

DR284

Contents

Preface

All of us hear the phrase, Where there's smoke, there's fire. This cliché implies that something greater, more serious, is behind the obvious smoke. We considered using the above cliché as the title for the book, but the title *Holy Smoke!* is a bit shorter—and we hope it communicates the same concept.

The idea of holy smoke comes from Leviticus 3:5, when Aaron's sons caused holy smoke to rise from the altar as an offering of pleasing odor to the Lord. Instead of destroying what was being sacrificed, the smoke was offered up to God so that the Almighty could transform the gift for a greater use. Yet holy smoke, which was used in many other sacrifices as well, meant even more than this. The sacrificial offering was a symbol that everything the worshiper owned was dedicated to God—even the life of the person making the sacrifice. The smoke was just a visible symbol of something more powerful and important.

The market has been flooded in recent years with books calling for radical change in the church to prepare it for the new millennium. Some authors point to statistics to say that "the sky is falling" on the church. Others point to other data and see a new spiritual awakening on the horizon. In this book, we simply state the need for the church to reexamine how it practices the faith if the church is going to thrive in the twenty-first century. However, HOLY SMOKE! is not about offering something new; rather, it calls readers to relearn lessons from the biblical sacrifices of yesterday. We invite the reader and the church to enter into a journey of discovering what 1000 B.C.E. (Before the Common Era) can teach us in 2000 C.E. (Common Era).

Christians are no longer called to devote themselves to creating holy smoke with the entrails of an animal. However, we believe that we are still equally called to give sacrificially. The tithe is a gift. It is a benchmark of giving that we are invited to offer up to the Lord for transformation to a greater good. By reclaiming the practice of tithing, along with other spiritual disciplines, the church will not only survive but also fulfill its mission in the twenty-first century—we are convinced of that.

But reclaiming spiritual disciplines will not be easy. A couple of years ago a good friend of ours was told by his doctor to either exercise or run the risk of losing his health. He began exercising the very next day but went painstakingly slow. When time came for exercise, his body cried out for the recliner. Priorities of time and money had to change. He fell off the wagon a couple of times; but after two years of consistent exercise, he is now running several miles a day and couldn't imagine his life without this discipline. He has become so faithful that some of his neighbors have become converts to running. Retraining ourselves to be stewards resembles this process. Stewardship is a process, and it takes time.

The stakes in encouraging and nurturing tithing are high, but they are well worth the effort. HOLY SMOKE! not only lays a historical and theological foundation for tithing but also gives a practical guide to follow in developing the discipline of systematic giving. Don't think for a moment that just reading this book will do the trick. Reading a book on tithing will not make you a generous person any more than reading a book on exercise will get you physically fit. If you follow through with the guide to holy smoke (tithing) offered in this book, however, our firm hope and prayer is that the fire will once again burn brightly in God's people and in God's church.

In the first chapter we offer a quick survey of current literature on giving, with a specific emphasis on giving to religion and to the church. This research was a major part of the motivation for us to write this book.

The second chapter seeks to lay out the biblical, historical, and theological basis for our premise for HOLY SMOKE!

The third chapter places the previous information in the context of the twentieth century as a way to answer the questions being asked about tithing in today's church. Some readers might consider this chapter our "apologetic" for tithing.

The fourth chapter presents a practical guide for any congregation that is open to becoming intentional about exploring holy smoke and the spiritual discipline of tithing.

The fifth and sixth chapters deal with what we call the "other pockets" of giving: planned giving and capital giving. Both of these have implications for the tither and for those seeking to practice holy smoke.

The two appendices relate to the process outlined in Chapter 4.

Go, and make holy smoke!

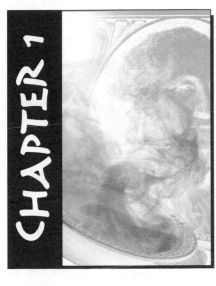

CHAPTER 1

Holy $moke!
What Is Happening to Giving Today?

I will offer to you burnt offerings of fatlings,
with the smoke of the sacrifice of rams;
I will make an offering of bulls and goats.

(Psalm 66:15)

A Tale of Holy $moke

It was a day that I shall never forget. At the tender age of twelve I was cooking my first meat loaf at home. All boys in my grade took six weeks of home economics. One project was to make a meat loaf. We practiced putting all the various ingredients into ground beef and rolling the mixture into a football-looking object. One afternoon I came home from school and thought I should practice my home economics skills. I discovered some ground beef in the refrigerator. I also found the mustard, onions, bread crumbs, ketchup, salt, and pepper. With great skill I rolled the ingredients into a masterpiece.

In class we ran out of time to get to the oven part; but I thought it shouldn't be too hard. I turned the oven to a temperature somewhere past halfway and placed a sheet of aluminum foil over the rack. No one told me that a pan should be used. I thought doing a meat loaf was sort of like doing a big steak on the grill.

About ten minutes into the process, smoke started rolling from the oven—lots and lots of smoke. Something was wrong! Soon the entire kitchen and most of the house filled with smoke. After fighting my way through the haze, I turned the oven off and opened the door. Whoa! The smoke was coming from the fat that hit the bottom of the oven. I pulled the meat loaf out of the oven about the time my father walked into the house from work. "Holy smoke, son! What are you doing?" he exclaimed. His use of holy must have given me a quick answer; for, remembering one of my Sunday school lessons, I replied, "I am making sacrifices to God. This is a burnt offering."

My answer didn't fly. I received paternal retribution for nearly burning down the house. I promised never to do it again.

This silly childhood story may be closer than we want to admit to the understanding most of us have of making a sacrifice unto God. The concept of *sacrifice* has become something of a household joke rather than denoting a relationship with God. "Holy smoke" seems quaint—and the mission of the church may be suffering because of it. Christians today can learn from the presentation of burnt offerings made to the Lord by our ancestors and can grow in our relationships with all of God's creation.

God invited the early Hebrews into a close personal relationship. Out of gratitude the Hebrew people looked for an appropriate way to affirm that relationship. The tithe was a culturally known act that was big enough to be significant. It was risky. It was sacrificial. Few could give ten percent of their crop or livestock without noticing it. To tithe their livelihood was a meaningful act of response to God for what God had done for them.

Even though it was common in that day and time to offer burnt offering as holy smoke, we should not assume that it was a trite ceremony. The Hebrews' offering of tangible value was freely given. The smoke wafted to the heavens with the hope that God might transform the gift for higher purposes. The great transformation, of course, happened not in the gift (smoke) but in the giver. Giving sacrificially did not make the Hebrew people religious, but the holy smoke became an important sign: If the people of God could not sacrifice holy smoke, then how could God expect to count on them within a world in need of transformation? Holy smoke was one of the disciplines by which the Hebrew people could measure their spiritual health. Without the relationship to God, the smoke was merely a foul-smelling fire.

Many contemporary measurements of the spiritual health of churches in North America raise serious concerns. Thomas Edward Frank has confessionally described the contemporary church as "immersed . . . in a rhetoric of crisis."[1] We do not want to get caught up with the alarmists who believe that the sky is falling. We are not card-carrying members of "doomsayers international"; nor are we pleased with everything we see. Every age presents new choices. The dilemmas of the church provide us with alternatives. We can either describe what we see as smudge pots trying to keep away the damage of a hard freeze or as a divine call for holy smoke.

In the midst of the variety of voices, it is clear that tithing is a hot button to some people and a total mystery to others. We meet people who swear by it, others who swear at it, and still others who haven't the foggiest idea how *tithing* is pronounced.

In this book, we propose a renewed look at tithing as a means of symbolizing and renewing the Christian's relationship with God. When we offer

---

1 From *Policy, Practice, and Mission of The United Methodist Church,* by Thomas Edward Frank (Abingdon Press, 1997); page 21.

God that which is precious to us, we are getting serious about our relationships. This book is about having fun while getting serious about a closer relationship with God through Jesus Christ.

Measuring the $moke

Faith is not a detached reality; it is the way we sort out meaning in life. It touches every part of who we are. It is connected to our personal and family decisions and to the institutions that are part of the real stuff of daily living. One relationship that has been central to Christian people from early times is the gathered community, the church. The church is an instrument for renewing the faith and hope of the believer; for sharing the good news with others; for feeding the hungry, healing the sick, clothing those without clothes, and providing shelter for those who have none. With that purpose and meaning, it seems strange that in these thriving economic times, a declining portion of church members' financial resources are offered through the church.

Giving is a measure—a sign—of the believer's and the gathered community's spiritual pulse. It is not the only measure of the church's effectiveness, but its significance cannot be disregarded in our North American economic system.

During the last decade of the twentieth century, new books about church giving seemed to proliferate. *Behind the Stained Glass Windows*, by John and Sylvia Ronsvalle, sparked vigorous debate in religious journals. The authors scanned the current religious horizon in North America from Catholic to mainline Protestant to evangelical to Pentecostal in order to understand attitudes and practices about giving and church finance. Some denominational leaders they interviewed vigorously affirmed tithing, others argued against it, and some were silent on the subject. However, only six pages in their book of more than three hundred pages discuss tithing.[2]

A consistent cord throughout the Ronsvalles' book is the desire by church leaders for believers to bring the entire scope of their (economic) life under the lordship of Christ. Even leaders uncomfortable with the practice of tithing base their opposition primarily on the ways tithing has been promoted up to the present era. Both advocates of tithing and those who are either reluctant or opposed to the encouragement of tithing tend to couch the debate in either/or terms: Is the tithe a symbol of one's total commitment, or is it a convenient transaction with God so that people can be absolved from guilt over the way they spend the other ninety percent? We are not comfortable with the line drawn in the sand. Symbolism and reality need to go together.

---

2 *Behind the Stained Glass Windows: Money Dynamics in the Church*, by John Ronsvalle and Sylvia Ronsvalle (Baker Books, 1996); pages 187–193.

Many people equate tithing with duty and obligation. "Ten percent" comes across as a heavy burden, resembling compulsory taxation. Unfortunately, the tithe is often promoted as duty in ways that fit neither our contemporary view of God nor our experience of relying upon God's grace. However, we will make a case that people both desire and need disciplines and guidelines. Christian disciples require benchmarks or mile markers along the pilgrimage of life. We believe that the tithe is a Christian's most helpful benchmark for financial giving.

The Ronsvalle book grew out of their research on the state of church giving. In *The State of Church Giving through 1995*, the Ronsvalles tracked the continuing decrease in giving to the institutional church as a percentage of income by church members. They discovered declines every year since 1968. During that period of time, ". . . church member giving increased by 33%" and "the portion of income donated to the church declined by 21%."[3] The erosion is evident in both mainline and evangelical denominations. In fact, the evangelical denominations are closing the gap (in a negative way) with the mainliners. A smaller and smaller proportion of people's resources is being offered up as holy smoke. No one can claim that tithing is a current fad.

Ronald Vallet and Charles Zech had an attentive audience for their book with the ominous title *The Mainline Church's Funding Crisis*. In a 165-page analysis of the severe decline in denominational funding, along with theological reflection, they devoted only half a page to tithing, and it came near the end of their book. Essentially, Vallet and Zech discredit the tithe as a standard of giving in favor of looking at one hundred percent.[4] Although we agree with the overall premise, we maintain that the new believer (and new giver) hasn't a clue about a way to translate these authors' eloquent phrases into a decision about what to put into the plate during a Sunday worship service. People need benchmarks. To proclaim that all we are and all we have belongs to the Lord does not help the person know what dollar amount to write on the church check.

In 1997, Robert Wuthnow wrote a book titled *The Crisis in the Churches: Spiritual Malaise, Fiscal Woe*. In it, he builds a case that the fiscal problems faced by congregations are primarily spiritual issues. We agree. However, in his well-written book, Wuthnow dedicates only two pages, plus a few other passing comments, to tithing. In a brief anecdotal reference, Wuthnow points out that the decision to tithe may be a major act of faith for some individuals.[5] We regret that he did not say that the decision to tithe is a sig-

3 From *The State of Church Giving through 1995*, by John Ronsvalle and Sylvia Ronsvalle (empty tomb, inc., 1997); page 92.

4 *The Mainline Church's Funding Crisis: Issues and Possibilities*, by Ronald E. Vallet and Charles E. Zech (William B. Eerdmans Publishing Company, 1995).

5 *The Crisis in the Churches: Spiritual Malaise, Fiscal Woe*, by Robert Wuthnow (Oxford University Press, 1997); page 73.

nificant decision for *most* of the individuals who make it. Tithing is a powerful symbol of the priorities in the giver's life.

Wuthnow is on the right track. We wish he had expanded upon his own statement. Our churches and our society require symbols for good. We believe that tithing can be a tangible sign along the pathway out of the apparent malaise.

Denominational committees, seeking to stem the attrition in their revenues, pore through the research of Dean Hoge and others. What is causing the decline in the percentage of income given? Church leaders want to know. In fact, the research group that produced *Money Matters* talked to a wide range of clergy about tithing. By and large they discovered that most clergy are uncomfortable with saying much about the subject. The authors' conclusion is that ". . . the issue of tithing is a matter of strength and type of personal faith."[6]

This statement by the research team seems to be a serious indictment of clergy in America. One's personal faith is evident in the way money is saved, spent, invested, and given. Hoge and his associates imply that neither spiritual nurture in the churches nor clergy education in seminaries has known what to do with the matter of tithing. The discomfort is a sign of need. Someone needs to address the issue. We suspect that the problem is not tithing but the entire relationship to money, and that silence about tithing is symptomatic of the problem. But ignoring the symptom doesn't make the problem go away.

In their follow-up book *Plain Talk About Churches and Money*, Hoge and his colleagues give little attention to tithing. In a review of giving in contemporary North America, they briefly report on the historical practice of tithing among Mormons and the Assemblies of God. In their assessment of both of those groups, the tithe is seen as a kind of tax imposed by God on the believer.[7] As near as we can tell, it is discounted as a symbol of one's relationship with God.

George Barna and his research firm work primarily with evangelical and conservative churches and parachurch groups. His recent book *How to Increase Giving in Your Church* (Regal Books, 1997) includes a significant amount of data about giving in North America. He has more to say about tithing than most other authors we surveyed. His book is important for giving a fuller view of the North American picture of church giving.

Barna's research is not much more encouraging than the others. He discovered that only "one-third of all born-again Christians who attend a

6 Reproduced from *Money Matters*, by Dean R. Hoge, Charles Zech, Patrick McNamara, and Michael J. Donahue. Copyright 1996 Westminster John Knox Press. Used by permission of Westminster John Knox Press; page 151.

7 *Plain Talk About Churches and Money*, by Dean Hoge, Patrick McNamara, and Charles Zech (The Alban Institute, Inc., 1997).

church" even believe that the Bible teaches tithing.[8] Only a small percentage of those who think tithing is taught actually do it. It appears that many contemporary Christians have decided that the tithe is a relic of the past.

From this brief survey, it is obvious that tithing is not a bandwagon issue. Proposing a fresh look at tithing may seem like an attempt to swim against the tide. So be it. Christian faith and action have a long history of doing just that. We invite you to join us in the swim.

The New Age May Drive Us to an Old Custom

A new generation is coming into the churches. It needs specific help in how to grow in the faith. The silence about tithing on the part of authors who write about giving, and on the part of pastors in local congregations, as well as their ambiguity about marks of discipleship, do not serve us well. Benchmarks are helpful! One of those helpful benchmarks is the tithe.

In spite of the widespread silence about tithing, some church leaders *are* speaking up. We join their appeal for a fresh look at this ancient practice. There are several reasons why a new openness is developing. Some are spiritual; others are pragmatic. Simply put, many churches are experiencing financial distress. Church expense ratios have undergone major shifts; at the same time, subtle changes have occurred in the giving habits of church goers. For instance, costs of utilities increased dramatically in the 1970's with the OPEC oil embargo. Congregations were barely making the adjustment to the higher costs of heating, cooling, and lighting their buildings when insurance rates raced to new heights. The resulting financial crunch has caught the attention of all who care about the institutional church and its ministries.

While price adjustments have created havoc in the marketplace, the number of available volunteers has decreased. A larger percentage of women have taken regular employment outside the home. This has affected staffing in congregations. Part-time and full-time employees have been hired to replace the volunteers in order to maintain a comparable level of services.

At the same time, congregations seem to demand increased excellence. More costly buildings, more expensive paper for the church bulletin, additional electronic equipment, and a host of other items have collided with budget realities. Excellence, as part of the current cultural expectation, costs money—even in the church!

Smaller congregations are not exempt from the fiscal crunch. Increases in salaries and related benefits have priced many churches out of the market for a full-time pastor. They feel economically squeezed. Large

8 From *How to Increase Giving in Your Church*, copyright 1997 Regal Books, Ventura, CA 93003. Used with permission; page 85.

congregations look with jaundiced eyes at denominational budgets that include salary-support grants for smaller congregations. They believe that they are being asked to contribute to non-productive ministries. Clergy and lay leadership in the bigger churches argue that they could spend the funds given by the people in ways that produce more results (more members?) for the gospel.

Denominational leaders agonize over funding ministries beyond the local church. Smaller percentages of funds from the plate are forwarded to denominational ministries. As maintenance costs increase, denominational officials are having a harder and harder time making the case that the funds they receive are used for the mission of the church.

Cultural shifts also affect the ways people give. Designated giving attracts a more favorable response by the person in the pew than the anonymous and often mysterious "church budget." Individual decision-making is a maxim of the age. Many people feel uneasy about yielding decisions over the distribution of funds to a small group within the congregation called a committee on finance. Givers feel cut off from recipients rather than connected to them.

Trust is another major factor affecting contributions. Scandals hit the television and newspaper headlines. Givers demand accountability. "Trust us" doesn't work anymore. At every level of church life, there is no longer the presumption that the money will be used responsibly. Nothing lowers the level of giving more dramatically than the conviction that money is not used by the organization for its announced purposes.

All of these factors are dramatically shown in *Giving USA*, the annual report on philanthropy that is released by the AAFRC Trust for Philanthropy. Even though giving in North America continues to rise at a level above the cost of living, giving to religion as a percentage of these contributions has shown a decline for many years. Giving to religion used to be well over fifty percent of all gifts in North America; now it makes up approximately forty-five percent of the total. Local congregations and denominational officials will see few positive indicators in the trend lines.

The litany of financial pain goes on and on. In response to the pain experienced by the institutional church, a popular financial campaign program currently used in the congregations of mainline denominations urges a focus on the giver's need to give rather than on the church's need to receive money.[9] Giving is urged in order to address the spiritual health of the individual rather than to solve an institutional problem for the church. The campaign emphasis moves from the budget to the act of giving itself.

9 *Consecration Sunday Stewardship Program*, by Herb Miller (Abingdon Press, 1986, 1988, 1993, 1995); page 6. Available through Cokesbury.

The strongest proponent of the focus on the giver is Douglas M. Lawson, Ph.D., whose book *Give to Live: How Giving Can Change Your Life* was published in 1991.[10] Lawson emphasizes the physical, emotional, and spiritual benefits of giving both of one's time and of one's money. His book is about philanthropy rather than church finance, but a local-church campaign has been published using the book as a primary text.[11] Tithing is mentioned nowhere in the entire book. The focus is on generous giving, but there are no guidelines or benchmarks.

We affirm the shift away from focusing on the congregation's budget, but we believe that the Lawson book took the thesis too far. In some ways, focusing on the benefits to the giver only feeds into North American individualism. Although it moves us away from giving only for institutional preservation, we believe that the question needs to be recast. Holy smoke is necessary for the spiritual health of the giver *and* for the mission of the church. It is not "either/or" but "both/and." It is imperative that the spiritual health of the person and the mission of the church be centered in God.

To overstate our case a bit, we believe that the primary focus for giving in the Old Testament was God. The primary focus for the Ronsvalles is the need to feed starving children. The major emphasis of Lawson is the physical, emotional, and spiritual health of the individual.

Too often churches have centered on financial requirements to survive rather than on opportunities for ministry made possible by generous giving of the people. The aim of giving has frequently been funding the *budget* rather than enabling the preaching of the good news to the poor, proclaiming release to the captives and recovery of sight to the blind, and freeing the oppressed of the world (Luke 4:18). It has been giving without vision.

The tithes and offerings described in the Old Testament were used in many ways. Some were burned on the altars, making holy smoke that would waft to the heavens. Other tithes were gathered for feasting and partying. (See Deuteronomy 14:22-29.) The feasts recited the stories of God's saving acts in their history. According to Malachi 3:8-12, the tithes were put in storehouses and used as the economic safety net for the people of Israel. The tithes were the "food stamps" for the needy, because God was a God of justice and mercy.

Prophets decried ritual sacrifice that was not accompanied by direct service to those who were left out and cast aside by society. It was not one or the other. Piety and service were yoked together. Why claim that it is either tithing or giving one hundred percent? The tithe is a spiritual discipline to help us put the whole of life under the lordship of Jesus Christ. The ministries supported by tithes affect relationships in the whole community.

10 *Give to Live: How Giving Can Charge Your Life*, by Douglas M. Lawson, Ph.D. (ALTI Publishing, 1991).

11 The *Give to Live: A Program of Joyful Giving for the Local Church* campaign packet is available from Cokesbury.

Tithing in the Whole $cheme of Things

In the next chapter, we survey the biblical references to tithing. That review shows that the tithe usually supported the religious and national establishment. In addition to tithes, many kinds of offerings are named and advocated in the Old Testament. In the New Testament, substantial parts of Paul's letters either report on the collection he organized for the poor in Jerusalem or explicitly give directions for this special offering. (See Acts 11:28-30; 2 Corinthians 8 and 9.) If we were to use contemporary business-management language, we could say that the tithe was for the *common-cause* support of the institution and its mission, while the offerings were for *special-cause* concerns. Tithes usually went for continuing expenses; special offerings were in response to either a particular blessing or an explicit need.

Research indicates that many older adults are willing to fund the ongoing establishment (common-cause support) and often want to protect the congregation from special offerings. Young adults tend to appreciate the special offerings (special-cause support) but chafe at supporting the ongoing budgetary needs of the congregation and the denomination.

Tithing can be an important symbol for both young and old. Since the tithe is meant to be a symbol of one's relationship to God, no age is exempt. Spirituality may take different forms in different generations, but all people yearn for a relationship regardless of whether or not they can name the ache.

Our experience with young adults in North America gives us hope. Many have an openness to discussing spiritual matters. They react negatively to the "hard sell." They want to connect with God and with one another. For this reason, the tithe is a symbol they can embrace as a benchmark to work toward and to move beyond.

Many young adults have serious questions about the institutional church and, for that matter, all institutions. Humans live in the tension between the framework and opportunity that institutions provide, and the tendency of institutions to become rigid and stultifying. The church is not exempt. When symbols of growth become rules for spiritual judgmentalism, all suffer.

The tithe is a benchmark along a journey rather than a mark of having arrived at the destination. When we travel on highways today, we need roads, signposts, and other benchmarks such as motels, restaurants, and gas stations. These are institutions. Their purpose is to serve the public on its journey. Likewise, benchmarks such as tithing are required for the person on the spiritual journey.

Most readers of this book are likely to be heavily involved in the institutional life of the church. You care about it. We also care about it. It has ministered to us along our spiritual journey. Many if not most of our significant relationships are connected to the church. The temptation is strong to approach the issue of tithing from the standpoint of the church's need for money to operate its budget. The institution needs money to continue. We want the institution to continue. Seductive pressures entice us to direct our attention to those institutional concerns rather than to the question of *why* we give. We can even make good arguments for doing so. Significant moral and ethical issues affect our decisions about where to direct our tithes and offerings. We do not want to diminish these. Pearls are not to be cast before swine.

At the heart of the matter is a spiritual issue: Whom do we serve? What are the ways we can express our allegiance to God? What is important to God?

Each day we make choices. The consequence of our choices is not primarily economic but relational. We dare to claim that the consequences are also eternal. After all, where our treasure is, there our hearts are also (see Matthew 6:21). Tithing is a helpful benchmark in the process of reordering our lives.

Instead of Burning Fat, We Are Getting Fat

Through instructing the band of "chosen people" to regularly bring sacrifices to the Lord, the Hebrew God got their attention. The smoke rising to the heavens reminded them of who God was and whose they were. Tithing is an attention-getting device. It is a remembering action.

There is an old story about a mule driver who preached gentleness but "got the mule's attention" by hitting the animal with a plank on the side of the head. Then he would gently give the mule directions. In some ways, the perceived fiscal woes of the churches may be the proverbial plank at the side of the head. They are a wake-up call. But tithing is not a gimmick to solve the economic problems of churches; it is a significant act of remembering who we are.

The tithe is not a deal we cut with God in order to assure our salvation. Instead, tithing is a blessed guide in an era when disciplines are relegated to fads rather than to normative behavior. Without discipline we forget who we are. Absence of discipline allows us in the church to get lazy. Tithing is a useful factor toward regaining spiritual fitness.

Spiritual fitness is not akin to muscle-flexing on the beach. It is about equipping people for mission in the rough and tumble of life. The venerable eighteenth-century church leader John Wesley called upon his followers to "reform the nation . . . and to spread scriptural holiness over the land."[12] In Paul's terms, we are to "put on the whole armor of God" (Ephesians 6:11). When people give, it is for that mission.

Tithing does not answer the question, Why give? It gets us to the practical question, How much shall I give? Businesses all across the world are

---

12 From "Minutes of Several Conversations Between the Rev. Mr. Wesley and Others. From the Year 1744, to the Year 1789," *The Works of John Wesley on Compact Disc*, Volume Eight (Providence House Publishers, 1995); page 299.

discovering the value of benchmarks. Throughout history, faith communities have recognized the need for benchmarks. Recently such specific practices and signs have been ignored or downplayed by many churches. A laissez faire attitude has taken over the church as well as the marketplace. The idea that possessions might be the subject of church discipline seems almost un-American.

God's children in God's church are called to be strong. In this book we appeal to believers to reclaim some of the power of the faith by reclaiming the call to make holy smoke—sacrifices surrendered unto God. A significant financial benchmark on the journey toward spiritual strength is the tithe.

The economic crunch experienced by both congregations and judicatories at the close of the twentieth century alerts us to the low set of expectations in most congregations. Even in many congregations that count on frequent attendance at worship and that urge regular study of the Bible, little is said about economics. The ways we earn money, the values that guide our management of funds, and the distribution of our financial resources are all important faith-related issues. We cannot be faithful and remain silent at the same time.

The discipline of tithing is a blessed gift to help individual Christians order their entire economic life. Few of us would doubt that we need such ordering when it comes to our checkbooks and credit card bills. Those who claim that the issue is not about giving ten percent but rather about giving one hundred percent are correct. That is why we see the tithe as a helpful benchmark in the pilgrimage *toward* full discipleship, where one hundred percent of what we have and what we are is under the lordship of Jesus Christ. The tithe is not the end of the person's responsibility. Just as Moses followed holy smoke (a pillar of cloud) across the desert, so the tithe can be a guide to our decision-making in the economic pilgrimage of life. It is a guide, not a goal.

The tithe is not the only benchmark for giving listed in the Bible, but it is the most consistent one. However, once a person or family reaches that benchmark, another basis is needed. Jesus affirmed, inspired, and called people to go beyond the tithe. One time, he invited himself to dinner at the home of a tax collector named Zacchaeus. We don't have any record of the conversation, but we know that after the meal with Jesus, Zacchaeus announced his decision to give away fifty percent of his possessions (Luke 19:1-10). Jesus asked a wealthy young ruler to give one hundred percent (Luke 18:18-25). A widow in the Temple received the praise of Jesus for her gift of one hundred percent (Luke 21:1-4).

Ultimately, we all give one hundred percent. We are going to spend it or give it somewhere, sometime. We do not take it with us. We are created to

An ecumenical group interviewed a potential author for a book on tithing. The author, a professor at a theological school, distributed an abstract for the book to the group and asked for feedback. The abstract had an academic feel to it. For about fifteen minutes the conversation droned on at a scholarly level. Finally, a lanky layman from California leaned over the table and said, "Doctor, I would like to know: Do you tithe?" The professor quickly responded, "Yes, I do." Then, after a pause he added, ". . . but I never intended to." He had everyone's attention as he went on to tell his story. "I never thought much about tithing," the professor said. "I never set the tithe as a goal for my giving. However, a few years ago while figuring my income tax, I realized that I had been tithing for several years. It wasn't something I tried to do. It was a result of a change of priorities in my life."

give. When giving is freely chosen, it is a beautiful human response to grace. The tithe provides guidance for that response.

Is tithing a spiritual issue, an issue of personal values, an institution issue, a mission concern, all of the above, or none of the above? At various times in history, one or another of these factors has been primary. We believe that it is important to see the variety of factors in creative tension. For us, it is all of the above! When separated from spirituality, tithing becomes a manipulative fundraising tool. When separated from personal values, it becomes a calculated deal with God. When separated from the life of institutions, it denies the incarnational dimension of our discipleship. When separated from the personal and institutional mission, it loses its focus.

For some people, the discipline of tithing leads to new priorities. For others, new priorities lead to tithing. We cannot prescribe one method for God to work or for people to respond. We can only share what we have experienced.

God has been good to the two of us. We have been blessed far beyond our deserving—even in material ways. We are not rich, but we have "enough." We have experienced grace. Parents, spouses, church leaders, and other mentors in our lives taught us to give in response to the gift of God's Son as well as in acknowledgment of life's other blessings. We are thankful! We know that we need to give in order to be whole. We are called to be part of a mission bigger than our family, our congregation, or our own lifetimes. Money is part of participating in that "bigger."

You are invited to join us in the pilgrimage—the discipline—of restoring tithing as a benchmark for giving in the life of the believer within the Christian community. To be transformed, we need to make holy smoke. Anything less is just burned meat loaf!

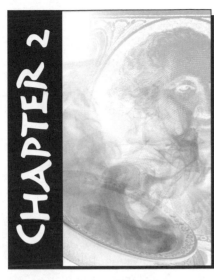

CHAPTER 2

A History of Holy $moke

*What shall I return to the LORD
for all his bounty to me?*

(*Psalm* 116:12)

How does a believer respond to God's goodness and mercy? Every person of faith struggles with this dilemma. What is appropriate? What does God want us to do? How can we experience a connection with the One who has given us life and hope? In this chapter, we explore ways in which the biblical writers wrestled with such questions. And, as we will see, time after time the tithe seemed to have been a part of their response.

The Tithe Before Abraham

The tradition of tithing has deep roots in the Old Testament. In fact, there is good evidence that tithing preceded the Hebrew people. In the fourteenth century before Christ, the tithe is found in Ugarit in the Syro-Palestine area. Nearly every primitive society made gifts to its god or gods. Usually those gifts were made with agricultural products, since primitive societies were predominantly agrarian. The size of the gift generally started out as one tenth of the crop. Later, the tenth new birth among the flocks and herds was sacrificed. This common practice in the ancient world took on distinctive forms appropriate to the culture in which it took root.

Both the Babylonians and the Egyptians tithed prior to the beginning of the practice among the Hebrews. Old records indicate that many early cultures expected to make an offering of one tenth of the spoils of war to some god. In the Greek legend of Hercules, Cacus stole Hercules' oxen. When Hercules regained his herd, he built an altar in Rome and asked the people to consecrate their tithes there.

In his book *Revolutionizing Christian Stewardship for the 21st Century: Lessons From Copernicus*, Dan Dick describes another important root of tithing:

Military historian William G. McGovern, in his book *Military Strate-gies of the Antiquities*, traces the notion of the tithe to ancient Egypt. McGovern claims that in Egyptian numerology, the number ten was a sacred and powerful number. It was the number of wholeness and completion. Soldiers were models of perfection physically, mentally, and emotionally. To be a soldier in ancient Egypt implied that one was a "perfect ten." When warriors went into battle, it was believed that they could continue to fight until they had received injury to a tenth part (a tithe) of their being. Once "tithed," a sol-dier was made incomplete, injured to the point where he could no longer stand on his own feet to fight. His salvation became depen-dent upon another. The tithe was a point of no return. A warrior was still self-sufficient until he incurred injury to a tenth part of his being. Beyond that point, self-sufficiency ended. In religious obser-vance, the tithe was a voluntary act of humility, symbolizing the need for the power of a deity to ensure a person's salvation. To tithe was to put oneself at risk, to give up control, to acknowledge need-iness. For the Hebrew people, the tithe was a supreme act of faith that endorsed their belief that God would provide for them in time of need.[1]

This story is probably the most preachable illustration for the tithe that we have come across. Although it is pre-Christian, it gets to the heart of the spiritual understanding of benchmark giving. However, each culture seemed to work out its own meaning for the practice. We will turn our attention now to the ways that the holy smoke helped the Hebrew people focus on who God was and upon their relationship to God.

The Tithe and the Old Testament

Attempts to trace the practice of tithing through the Scriptures are a lit-tle like trying to follow the nuances and changes in the United States tax code. The path is not a direct route but a dynamic course of forming and reforming. We might desire a nice, linear progression in the tradition of tithing, but that's not the way it was. For example, the last chapter of Leviti-cus (chapter 27) describes one kind of tithe, while Numbers 18:21-32 tells of another tithe (or system of tithing) to support the Levites and local sanc-tuaries. However, the directions for the tithes are nearly identical in Deuteronomy 14:22-29 and Deuteronomy 26:1-15.

In the third and sixth years of a six-year cycle, apparently the tithe was to go for strangers, orphans, widows, and others who were cut off from the economic mainstream. (See Deuteronomy 14:27-29.) During the remaining

---

1 From *Revolutionizing Christian Stewardship for the 21st Century: Lessons From Copernicus*, by Dan R. Dick (Discipleship Resources, 1997); pages 44–45.

years, the faithful Hebrew would bring the tithe to a holiday banquet.

To add to the complexity, there were variations in what was to be tithed. Most of the tithes were based on crops. Deuteronomy 14, for example, lists new grain, wine, and oil. Cattle as a tithe are mentioned only in Leviticus 27:32-33.

So the common question of our day—How do we figure the tithe?—has roots back in ancient times; however, arguments about the base for tithing continue. A few writers today try to make a coherent pattern out of the variety of Old Testament traditions, while others simply ignore any part of the biblical tradition that does not fit the situation in their own culture. One thing is for certain: The biblical stories that provide the sources of our inquiry about tithing are fascinating but confusing.

But confusion and complexity are no reason for not plumbing the rich biblical sources for insight about tithing; so, let's press on. One of the clearest descriptions of the tithe is found in the apocryphal book Tobit. Tobit says:

> I would hurry off to Jerusalem with the first fruits of the crops and the firstlings of the flock, the tithes of the cattle, and the first shearings of the sheep. I would give these to the priests, the sons of Aaron, at the altar; likewise the tenth of the grain, wine, olive oil, pomegranates, figs, and the rest of the fruits to the sons of Levi who ministered at Jerusalem. Also for six years I would save up a second tenth in money and go and distribute it in Jerusalem. A third tenth I would give to the orphans and widows and to the converts who had attached themselves to Israel. I would bring it and give it to them in the third year, and we would eat it according to the ordinance decreed concerning it in the law of Moses.
>
> (Tobit 1:6b-8, Apocrypha)

In the canonical Scriptures the first description of tithing follows an interesting war story described by the writer of Genesis. A group of marauding kings (tribal chiefs) raided Sodom and carried off Lot and his family. Abram gathered an army and went after the marauders. He chased them for about one hundred miles, engaged them in combat, and won the battle. On the way home, his route took him through Salem, the home of Melchizedek, a king and high priest. King Melchizedek did the hospitable thing expected in that culture: He presented the weary warriors with bread and wine. In response to the act of hospitality, Abram offered one tenth of his spoils of war to King Melchizedek. (See Genesis 14.)

We would be hard-pressed to claim that this normal act of Middle Eastern hospitality was a law for Christians or Jews. No pietistic dimension is suggested by the Genesis story. It may have been no more religious than the practice in many parts of North America of taking a house-warming gift when joining a family for dinner in their home. Nor did Abram give Melchizedek any of his own personal flocks, crops, or property; he gave a portion of the spoils of battle. Furthermore, there is no record of Abram ever again giving an offering to Melchizedek.

The next recorded incidence of tithing in the Bible takes place when Abraham's grandson Jacob fled to Haran after a quarrel with this brother, Esau. Jacob had a traumatic night at a place named Bethel. After an all-night wrestling match with a heavenly being, he built an altar and tried to make a bargain with God. Jacob promised that if God would care for him, and if he were to prosper, he would give one tenth. (See Genesis 28.) From our perspective, his bargaining sounds like the description of contract negotiations resulting in the agent receiving a ten percent commission. Additionally, there is no record in the Bible that Jacob ever paid his end of the bargain. He did prosper, but there is a strange silence about any offering.

During the entire pivotal story of Israel's escape from Egyptian bondage, the only reference to the tithe is found in Leviticus 27. Some four hundred years after Jacob made his bargain with God at Bethel, the act of giving one tenth was codified into Hebrew law. Leviticus 27:30-33 orders the tithe as an act of remembrance of God's ownership. Every tenth lamb to be born and every tenth bushel of grain harvested was to be given. The tithe legislation included all agricultural produce.

We also find a catalog of offerings in Leviticus 27 (verses 1-29) that sounds similar to a recitation of head taxes and land-transfer fees. In addition to the tithe and offerings, the jubilee is described in this chapter (verses 17-25). The jubilee was a celebration that took place every fifty years and during which all debts were forgiven and all slaves freed. That radical concept is ignored by almost all contemporary Christians, even though there is more said about the jubilee than about tithing in Leviticus 27.

In the instructions for building the Tabernacle in Exodus 35:4-35, no mention is made of the tithe. During the entire forty-year trek across the wilderness, there is no description of tithing. It was not until the Israelites entered the Promised Land and settled there that new rules for living were needed. One of those rules was the tithe.

The Book of Numbers (18:20-32) makes mention of the need for another law in response to the new situation facing the Israelites upon entering the land of promise, Canaan. Hebrew leaders parceled out the territory to eleven of the twelve tribes. Levites were to administer the "tent of meeting" (the sanctuary) and therefore did not receive any land to farm. Instead, they were to receive one tenth (a tithe) of the crops and one out of ten new births from the herds of the other eleven tribes. This tithe was to support the religious establishment of the day, but it did more than that. In addition to religious ceremonial obligations, the Levites also had civil responsibilities.

Thus, the tithe was also a tax to support the civil and religious infrastructure of the fledgling nation.

Deuteronomy 12 and 14 provide an additional snapshot of the practice of tithing among the Israelites. For the first time, money is mentioned in connection with sacrifices and offerings. The tithe of grain or wine, or a portion of the herds, was to be brought to "the place that the LORD your God will choose" (Deuteronomy 12:5). However, transporting flocks and bushels of grain could be a logistical problem. In cases where transporting the tithe would be a hardship, the produce or livestock could be sold and converted to money, and the money brought to the place that God had chosen for the annual gathering. Once there, the money could be converted into food and drink for a time of celebration (Deuteronomy 14:22-26).

Both Deuteronomy 12 and 14 include a fascinating description of the annual festival. The tithe becomes the opportunity and symbol for a great time of feasting and celebration. The Israelites had a multi-day party! The festive atmosphere stands in sharp contrast to much of the somber, hard-driven advocacy of tithing we sometimes hear in the present day.

The final mention of tithing in the Pentateuch (the first five books of the Old Testament) is found in Deuteronomy 26:1-15. The passage wonderfully recounts the story of Israel's formation and their salvation from Egyptian bondage. Specific directions outline both the offerings and the tithes, as well as the way in which these were to be presented. The passage ends with the statement: "Look down from your holy habitation, from heaven, and bless your people Israel and the ground that you have given us . . ." (26:15). One could interpret this statement to mean: "We are grateful, God. You did what You promised to do. We have done what we were to do—we gave our tenth. Now it's your turn again. Please bless us."

Except for the Deuteronomy 26 passage, all other references in the Torah specify *how* the tithe is to be collected and distributed; that is, there was no need to make a case for the tithe. It was assumed to be part of the life of the Hebrew people. The passages merely clarified the rules for tithing in this fledgling nation.

As we continue our journey through the Old Testament, we come to the time when the people of Israel pleaded for a king. They wanted to be like other nations. Samuel told them it would cost them. In fact, he said they would have to ante up another ten percent to support a king (1 Samuel 8:15-17). In this instance, the tithe was clearly a civil tax and had nothing to do with feeding the poor or keeping the priesthood functioning. In fact, some scholars believe that the actual amount of this "tithe" was more than ten percent.

When King Hezekiah began an important reform of Israel during his reign, he called upon the people to restore a practice that seemed to have been forgotten. Judging from 2 Chronicles 31:4-12, it appears that the tithe had two purposes: first, to support the priests and Levites (verse 4); and second, as a visible symbol of dedication of the people to God (verse 10).

Another story of restoration is recorded in Nehemiah. The Israelites had come back from exile in Babylon. Nehemiah headed up the building project to rebuild the Jerusalem wall. Tithes were commanded to be brought to Jerusalem—but primarily to support the Levitical priesthood. (See Nehemiah 10, 12, and 13.)

The prophets also mentioned tithing. It is not hard to visualize a sneer on the lips of Amos as he condemns the people for bringing their tithes but not changing their ways (Amos 4:4-5). A tithe was not a way to wipe away evil deeds. Motivation seemed to be more important than calculation.

No passage gets quoted more often or more vigorously by advocates of tithing than Malachi 3:6-12. The denunciation of those who are not giving their full tithe is the fifth in a series of disputations by the prophet. In this prophetic book, post-exilic Israel is vigorously called to repentance. In his commentary on Malachi, Andrew Hill states that "the essential message of this penultimate oracle is repentance, not tithing. God wants honest and genuine worship from his people, of which tithing is but a symbol." [2] We wish Professor Hill had dropped the word *but* from his text. The oracle is a call to repentance and tithing; it is a symbol of worship of Yahweh's people. Malachi addresses the primary issue of the oracle in verse 7 of chapter 3: "Return to me . . ." Tithing is not a payoff to keep Yahweh at arm's length; tithing is a symbol of a personal relationship between the people and God.

Controversy has stormed around the words that Malachi attributes to God: "Put me to the test " (verse 10). Paul exhorts us, "We must not put Christ to the test" (1 Corinthians 10:9). We have two options for the interpretation of these conflicting verses: Either the two biblical writers disagree, or they mean different things by *test*. Paul seems to object to testing as people's spiritual "sting operation" to see if God really loves them. They want to know how much they can get away with and still be loved by God.

In other cases (including the pericope from Malachi 3), *test* refers to a discipline that cleanses the person and strengthens the relationship. The tithe is not the final seal of one's relationship with God. Rather, in these cases the tithe was "an appropriate first step in moving toward a relationship of fidelity with Yahweh because it necessitated a demonstration of faith in relinquishing already scarce staples . . ." [3] Likewise, we affirm the need for "first steps" today. Setting the tithe as a benchmark for giving seems an appropriate first step in a culture afflicted with "affluenza."

2 From *The Anchor Bible: Malachi: A New Translation with Introduction and Commentary*, by Andrew E. Hill (Doubleday, 1998); page 293.

3 From *The Anchor Bible: Malachi*, page 324.

We acknowledge and regret that Malachi 3:6-12 has often been used as a club to coerce people into tithing. To use the passage as legislation to demand tithing for all time is a case of selective biblical proof-texting. Malachi does chastise the people, to be sure; but it is for being out of relationship with God—of which the failure to tithe is a symptom.

Malachi condemns the people for not bringing tithes, but also for not bringing their offerings. For the Hebrew people, the rebuke includes sin offerings, thank offerings, and a profusion of other offerings described in the Scriptures. Most tithing legalists want to praise anyone who tithes and to affirm any additional offerings as acts of merit over and above the call of duty. They ignore the fact that the offerings were also commanded in the same breath as the tithe. If the Jewish tithe is commanded of all Christians, why are not all of the offerings mentioned in the Old Testament also required? Both tithes and offerings were symbols of Israel's relationship with God.

Malachi's message contains both curse and blessing. Tithing is vigorously affirmed. A covenant relationship with Yahweh promises a wonderful vision of plenty for all. Tithing is not the reason for the blessing but the symbol of the relationship. North American individualists often interpret the passage to mean that if you tithe, God will make you rich. An accurate reading of the passage indicates that a nation that tithes will be a nation where the number-one issue is its relationship with God. In such a place, everyone has enough and more. We can speculate that the prophet is claiming that those who tithe tend to have different priorities and will look after the needs of the greater community. The benefit is not individual but universal.

The tithe is a call to put God first rather than to place our own wants in front of everything. Now, wants are not bad. The problem is that we often *want* for the wrong things. God has called us to want for the health of the whole community. That does not align with the desire to accumulate as much as we can. Watching holy smoke can be an exercise in keeping perspective.

When God's people turn away from the worship of God, they turn to selfishness. We believe that generous giving is an antidote to selfishness—a cure for affluenza. Tithing is a guide—a benchmark—that God has given us to keep our perspectives in balance.

The Tithe and the New Testament

We now turn to the New Testament. Every time the Gospel writers recorded Jesus talking about tithing, he appeared to be admonishing tithers instead of chastising those who did not tithe. He condemned those who went to the extreme of tithing even their spices while neglecting decency to the least and the lost of the community. (See Matthew 23:23 and Luke 11:42.) Apparently, the practice that was borne in thankfulness had become a rigid legalism.

Jesus told the parable about a Pharisee and a tax collector who both went to the Temple to pray. The Pharisee reminded God of his good deeds: "I fast twice a week; I give a tenth of all my income" (Luke 18:12). The tax collector made no such claims; yet it was the tax collector who went away from the Temple justified (verse 14). The story is a vivid example of Jesus' alignment with the prophets who condemned tithing for show.

In the Gospels, when the tithe becomes a way of separating people from one another rather than a celebration of community, it is condemned. The Pharisee in the Temple used the tithe as a medal to be worn for admiration. He had forgotten the purpose behind the ancient symbol: true sacrifice expressing great love to God. The tithe was a measure, a benchmark, for the sacrifice. It would seem that the aim of those rebuked by Jesus was to prove who could make the biggest blaze, not who would offer the greatest love. Tithing became a contest over measurements rather than an act of worship.

As Paul went about his task of raising funds for the poor in Jerusalem, he never mentioned tithing. Second Corinthians 8 and 9 were fundraising appeals. Paul's request for contributions was based on a wholly different standard than the tithe. He appealed to the Corinthians for a "generous undertaking" (8:6) rather than a tithe. No reference was made to a percentage. The gift was to be based on the Corinthian believers' remembrance of what Jesus had done for them, along with the fact that they had something to give.

The argument has been made, and it certainly could be a valid one, that the reason Paul said so little to the early church about tithing was that it was already a standard practice for Jewish converts; moreover, the pressing need of the Gentile believers was to learn of the law of the Spirit, a greater law than the ancient laws written on parchment. Paul walked a fine line between the need for new Christians to learn discipline and practice holiness, and his concern that they not confuse such practices with legalism.

A few leaders in spiritual formation make a strong case that a close relationship with God almost always begins with a specific discipline. Early in the history of the Hebrew people, eight-day-old boys were brought to the Temple for circumcision—long before they could make any statement of faith. The same rationale is the foundation for infant baptism. The act precedes the understanding and personal appropriation of faith.

In the same way, people who want to develop a vibrant prayer life often begin with set times and practices. At some point in the process of maturation, these people discover that they "pray without ceasing" (1 Thessalonians 5:17). We suspect that there are many people who begin with the discipline of tithing and grow into generosity. Contentment in any discipline is an alarm bell for repentance rather than an excuse for pride.

Paul's great concern was for the health of the community of Jesus' people. If arrogance over some gift caused contention in the community of faith, the gift needed to be brought under the discipline of the community. We can surmise that a giver who lorded generous giving over the others was not helping the community of faith. Holy smoke was not a bragging right!

The Early Church and the Tithe

The history of tithing in the early church is a checkered one. Apart from the brief comments in the Gospels and Paul's silence about tithing, we find only one statement about tithing in all the rest of the New Testament. The Book of Hebrews refers to Abraham's gift (tithe) to Melchizedek (7:1-10). The seventh chapter of Hebrews is not an argument for the tithe but a carefully crafted case for Jesus being the great High Priest. Since our generation is not particularly awed by priests of any ilk, the whole argument seems a bit strange today.

Ten people gathered in a retreat center near Chicago late one Friday afternoon. After supper each person told his or her own story of giving.

Sunday morning the same group engaged in a study of 2 Corinthians 8. As they confronted verse 5 ("They gave themselves first to the Lord and, by the will of God, to us."), one participant noted the contrast between the chronology of their own stories and the order of events in Paul's letter: Unlike the believers in Macedonia, each of the Chicago group began giving before he or she made a profession of faith in Jesus Christ.

In wrestling with the mystery of this contrast in order, one of the group noted that Paul was writing to new converts, but that each person in the retreat group had grown up in the church. Then someone noted that some people who come into our church may be more like the Corinthian Christians—they have no history of giving—than like the group gathered for the weekend retreat.

Early-church leaders often advocated tithing; however, they were less likely to use legalism than they were to attempt to shame Christians into tithing. In the fourth century, John Chrysostom is recorded as saying, "[Jews] contributed tithes, and tithes again for the orphans, widows, and proselytes. Now, however, we are wont to hear such and such a one say with astonishment, 'So and so gives tithes!' How great a disgrace, I ask, is this: and what among the Jews was no matter of astonishment or celebrity, has now among Christians become a matter of surprise."[4]

Chrysostom's argument sounds similar to present-day denominational appeals that compare the giving of one denomination with another. For instance, United Methodists are challenged (embarrassed?) to give at least as well as the Presbyterians or the Lutherans. Episcopalians are urged to compare their giving with the Assemblies of God or Seventh-Day Adventists. Perhaps Jesus started the whole thing when he said, "Unless your righteousness exceeds that of the scribes and Pharisees, you will never enter the kingdom of heaven" (Matthew 5:20).

In a book written in 1909, John Wesley Duncan ascribes early writings about tithing to church fathers like Clement of Alexandria and Augustine of Hippo. Unfortunately, he does not footnote any of his references. He also quotes the Council of Trent (1545–1563):

> The payment of tithes is due to God; and they who refuse to pay them, or hinder those who give them, usurp the property of another. Wherefore, the holy Synod enjoins on all, of whatsoever rank and condition they be, to whom it belongs to pay tithes, that they henceforth pay in full the tithes, to which they are bound in law, to the cathedral church, or to whatsoever other churches, or persons, they are lawfully due. And they who either withhold them, or hinder them (from being paid), shall be excommunicated; nor be absolved from this crime, until after full restitution has been made.[5]

From Israel in the Old Testament through the Middle Ages, tithing was primarily an agrarian practice. As monetary systems developed, the practice moved to giving money rather than produce such as grain, oil, wine, or animals. In 1295 a provincial synod in London passed a law that

> tithes were to be paid on the gross value of all crops from the ground—from trees, herbs, and hay. It also set forth how tithes were to be paid on the produce on animals, lambs, and wool. The manner in which tithes on milk, fisheries, bees, and pasture of animals was to be estimated also was outlined in this canon. The most significant innovation, however, was the requirement of personal tithes—tithes on the profits of business, carpenters, blacksmiths, weavers, and all others working for wages.[6]

4 From *The Message of Stewardship: A Book for Daily Devotions and Class Study*, by Ralph Spaulding Cushman (Abingdon-Cokesbury Press, 1922); page 201.

5 From *Our Christian Stewardship*, by John Wesley Duncan (Jennings and Graham, 1909); page 66, as quoted from *The Canons and Decrees of the Sacred and Oecumenical Council of Trent Celebrated Under the Sovereign Pontiffs, Paul III, Julius III and Pius IV*, translated by The Reverend J. Waterworth (The Christian Symbolic Publication Society, 1848); page 269.

6 From "Stewardship in the History of the Christian Church," by Luther P. Powell, in *Stewardship in Contemporary Theology*, edited by T. K. Thompson. National Council of the Churches of Christ in the U.S.A. Copyright 1960. Used with permission. All rights reserved. Page 100.

European governments developed without the separation of church and state that we take for granted in the United States of America. The state acted as the agent of the church and included the tithe in the system of taxation. According to the *Encyclopaedia Judaica,* the tithe in Europe was similar to American real-estate and personal-property taxes.[7] Jewish property owners protested against paying taxes to support the church but apparently had little success. The government paid the bills of the church. Because political leaders often siphoned off a portion of the ten percent tithe-tax for civic and personal use, vigorous protests were common by church leaders.

Recent History

Little was said about the tithe among North American Christians until the late 1800's. A Presbyterian layman, Thomas Kane, along with Methodist and Presbyterian friends, started a powerful movement to advocate tithing.

> In 1870 Mr. Kane began to tithe his income, and after five years he noticed that his business had undergone a decided change for the better. Thereupon he began to make personal inquiries regarding the temporal prosperities of those who tithe, and he found almost complete agreement among tithers—tithing pays.[8]

The movement started by Kane reached its zenith in America in the period between 1890 and 1920. The group of men formed an organization named the Twentieth Century Tithe Covenant Association with offices in Indianapolis, Indiana. The strength of the association among Methodists appears to have been in Indiana, California, and Kansas, and among Presbyterians in Ohio and Illinois.

A colleague of Kane's, George W. Brown, compiled a vast assortment of sermons, testimonials, articles, and other statements in a book titled *Gems of Thought on Tithing: By Ministers and Laymen of All Denominations* (Jennings & Graham). The book, published in 1911, provides insight into the complexity of motivations behind advocates of tithing and the church culture of the time. The contributing writers are all over the theological spectrum. They represent a hodgepodge of understandings of tithing. The one thread of agreement is that every person quoted advocates tithing.

Brown states his rationale for the book in this way: "The long-neglected obedience to the tithe must again be restored to its rightful place in worship. Not in order to fill the treasuries, which in itself would be beneficial to the Church, but in order to win men (*sic*) away from covetousness and

---

7 *Encyclopaedia Judaica,* Volume 15; page 1162.

8 From *Stewardship in Contemporary Theology,* National Council of the Churches of Christ in the U.S.A. Copyright 1960. Used with permission. All rights reserved. Pages 121–122.

"In 1895 the pastor and three of the official members and their wives met to discuss the gloomy outlook for the Church. Everything had been tried but God's plan. It was suggested that they try the Bible method. This was met by one of the members, who stated that he had followed this method for years, but it was in a general way and given out by himself for many purposes, while the Scriptures declare the tithe is the Lord's, and should be brought into the storehouse.

They agreed to try this plan. A covenant was drafted and signed by those present . . .

At the close of the first year . . . the reports showed that for the first time in the history of the Church every obligation had been promptly met." [10]

selfishness and bring them to acknowledge God as the Supreme One . . ." [9] That argument appears many times in the book, but it is not the only one expressed; nor is it upheld by everyone quoted in the book.

It seems evident that many leaders within the tithing movement started by Kane wanted the church to focus on its mission rather than on fundraising. One fascinating argument put forth in *Gems of Thought on Tithing* condemns the variety of fundraising methods used to support the church's ministry:

Imagine the President of the United States and the committee on Ways and Means sending out jugs, mugs, boxes, barrels, eggs, and buttons with their pictures on them to catch pennies to meet the fiscal needs of the great government of the United States! Imagine the different States and counties holding fairs, festivals, concerns, ice-cream socials, with women cooking, sewing, and acting, that each community may meet its apportionment! This would disgrace any earthly government in its own and the eyes of the nations. Yet this is what Christians are doing year by year to finance the Kingdom of God. [11]

Rev. J. Whitcomb Brougher is quoted as advocating tithing as a means of decreasing denominational superstructure. He felt that if the money was not needed to promote giving, more would be available for missions. It is an

9 From *Gems of Thought on Tithing: By Ministers and Laymen of All Denominations*, compiled by George W. Brown (Jennings & Graham, 1911); page 163.

10 From *Our Christian Stewardship*; pages 112–115.

11 From *Gems of Thought on Tithing*; quotation by L. Wharton; page 145.

interesting concept. We doubt that it fully takes into consideration the doctrine of sin.

The covenant statement of Third Presbyterian Church in Chicago states, "That, having entered into this covenant, we will not be under obligation or expected to sign any other subscription or pledge of any kind for any Church work or benevolence."[12] It seems evident that many of the leaders in the tithing movement felt like they were being harassed for another contribution every time they turned around. Tithing was advocated to bring order out of the chaos.

Several contributors to *Gems of Thought on Tithing* testify to the way they financially prospered after they began tithing. The implicit argument is that tithing will end up making you money. This argument has roots in the Hebrew culture of Old Testament times. The Book of Proverbs seems to be a strong proponent of this position.

In 2 Kings 18, the writer describes the reign of Hezekiah. The king did all the right things, such as removing pagan altars. He "held fast to the LORD; . . . The LORD was with him; wherever he went, he prospered" (verses 6-7). The opposite side of the coin is described in Haggai: "You have looked for much, and, lo, it came to little; and when you brought it home, I blew it away. Why? says the LORD of hosts. Because my house lies in ruins, while all of you hurry off to your own houses" (Haggai 1:9).

Looking out for oneself rather than for the good of the community brings calamity, according to many biblical writers. Following God's call leads to prosperity. Another perspective is portrayed by Jeremiah in writing to the exiles in Babylon. In Jeremiah's understanding, the exiles were the "good guys"; yet they were going to have to endure an entire generational cycle (seventy years) as captives in a foreign land.

The same struggle about why bad things happen to good people is dealt with in dramatic fashion in the book of Job. The righteous man lost his health, his family, and his wealth. Throughout the Old Testament we see the Israelites trying to deal with the issue, What does it mean for God to bless? Does God's blessing mean prosperity? If so, why do such awful things happen to God's people?

The appeal to tithing as a route to prosperity has had an appeal throughout history. It points up a strange Catch-22. Those who tithe tend to bring the whole of their economic lives under greater discipline. The cultivation of new financial practices based on sound values often leads to prosperity. The prosperity then leads to pride and selfishness and results in a dimming of the flame of faith and ignoring the community of faith. We believe that those who hold the tithe as a *goal* to reach rather than as a *benchmark* for the

12 From *Gems of Thought on Tithing*, page 153.

"Does a person who tithes prosper more than one who does not tithe? I am not going to answer 'yes.' Prosperity means something other than material gain. As long as 'to be' is greater than 'to have' and 'to become' is greater than 'to get,' so long as will the greatest prosperity of life be inner growth, a thing of the heart." [13]

faith journey are particularly vulnerable to pride and self-centeredness.

We would not want to give the impression that all of the spokespeople for tithing around the turn of the century argued for tithing as a route to individual economic prosperity. Several contributors to *Gems of Thought on Tithing* clearly advocated for the need to practice Christian stewardship over one hundred percent of one's resources. Giving ten percent does not let one off the hook. So, for example, H. Clay Trumbell says that Christian stewardship applies to the use of the nine-tenths rather than to the tithe.[14]

Another contributor to *Gems of Thought on Tithing*, Rev. Willis L. Gelston, describes three different kinds of giving. The first is "haphazard giving." The giver gives whatever happens to be in the pants pocket at the time the offering is taken. He notes that haphazard givers usually think that they give more than they actually do.

The second kind of giving is tithing. In this, the giver figures out one tenth of the income and faithfully gives it. The third method Gelston calls stewardship giving. In it, the person examines how much is needed for personal and family living expenses; everything else is invested in ministry of Christ's kingdom.[15]

A curious reference to tithing appeared in *The Doctrines and Discipline of The Methodist Episcopal Church—1908*. Under a section titled "Special Advices," there is a paragraph named "Tithing." We quote the paragraph in full:

> We believe that the evangelization of mankind can best be accomplished by an adequate support of all the agencies used by the Church, and that to this end the scriptural doctrine of systematic giving should be taught in our pulpits and practiced by our ministers and members.[16]

---

13 From *The Minimum Standard of Giving*, by Earl G. Hamlett (Chicago: The General Board of Lay Activities, The Methodist Church, no date); page 8.

14 *Gems of Thought on Tithing*; page 153.

15 *Gems of Thought on Tithing*; pages 150–151.

16 From *The Doctrines and Discipline of The Methodist Episcopal Church—1908*, edited by Bishop Daniel A. Goodsell, Joseph B. Hingeley, and James M. Buckley (Eaton & Mains, 1908); pages 58–59.

Two comments seem appropriate. First, the word *doctrine* is used in a fairly sloppy manner. Tithing is many things, but it is not in the same category as the humanity and divinity of Jesus Christ. Doctrines are the kinds of things we find in the Apostles' Creed, but the judicial and ethical rules of the Scriptures are not appropriately called doctrines. Second, the heading for the section is "Tithing," but the word *tithe* is not used in the paragraph. We find that curious, to say the least.

We wish we knew details of the debate that surrounded the inclusion of the paragraph on tithing in the 1908 *Discipline;* we also wonder why the statement did not appear in the 1912 *Discipline* or subsequent *Disciplines.* The absence is probably another chapter in the age-old struggle between grace and legalism.

The fact that the paragraph was dropped after one quadrennium did not mean that tithing was a dead issue in The Methodist Episcopal Church. In 1919, Methodist bishop Ralph Spaulding Cushman strongly advocated tithing in a book titled *The New Christian: Studies in Stewardship.* Bishop Cushman said that "in the last analysis the call to pay the tithe is a call to trust in God in all fullness."[17] He did provide a caveat that would not please legalists when he said, "The setting apart of a definite proportion of income is of more importance than the exact determination of what that proportion of income shall be."[18]

In a later book, Bishop Cushman makes an interesting pragmatic argument for tithing. He argues that if more Christians had tithed and given their tithe to the church, more missionaries could have been sent to Japan. If more missionaries had gone to Japan, the attack on Pearl Harbor might have been averted.[19] That thesis sounds both triumphalistic and pompous for our ears, but we found it a fascinating merging of institutional concerns and patriotism.

Harvey Reeves Calkins, another Methodist, was a prolific advocate of tithing in the early part of the twentieth century. One of Calkins's arguments that appeals to us is his claim that tithing helps us experience God as personal rather than hold God aloof as an abstraction. He implies that when we lose the sense of a personal God, then we think in terms of what is *mine.* Things are known not for their intrinsic quality but by their owner. It is *my* house. *My* barns. *My* money. All sense of partnership and fellowship with God is lost.[20]

---

17 From *The New Christian: Studies in Stewardship,* by Ralph Spaulding Cushman (Centenary Conversation Committee, Methodist Episcopal Church, 1919); page 86.

18 From *The New Christian: Studies in Stewardship;* page 74.

19 *Will a Man Rob God? Four Studies in Christian Stewardship,* by Ralph Spaulding Cushman (Abingdon-Cokesbury Press, 1942); page 47.

20 *Stewardship Starting Points: An Introduction,* by Harvey Reeves Calkins (The Epworth League of The Methodist Episcopal Church, 1916).

After years of silence about tithing in any official documents of predecessor denominations of The United Methodist Church, it was not until 1988 that the General Conference inserted two new statements into the *Book of Discipline*. The first was placed in a section that defines the duties of local-church offices and groups. Chairpeople of the work area of stewardship have the responsibility for "informing them [church members] that tithing is the minimum goal of giving in The United Methodist Church."[21]

At the same General Conference, a similar phrase was inserted into the section in the *Discipline* on responsibilities for the annual conference stewardship unit. The conference unit is "to inform the local church that tithing is the minimum standard of giving in The United Methodist Church."[22]

Tithing advocates apparently worked hard on legislation for the 1988 General Conference, since they were also able to insert a resolution on tithing into *The Book of Resolutions of The United Methodist Church*.[23] The resolution was not dealt with at the 1996 General Conference, so it remains in the *Book of Resolutions*.

For nearly fifty years The Episcopal Church has made official statements about tithing. In the 1940 General Convention, church leaders stated: "We recognize that *tithing* is a definite, clear and practical method of establishing the base of a Christian's giving to religious, educational and charitable objects."[24] Fifteen years later, the Convention met in Honolulu, Hawaii, and passed another resolution on tithing. The Bishop of Chicago offered a resolution combining the personal and institutional reasons for tithing by affirming "the spiritual importance and personal need of tithing in order to expand the work of the Church at home and abroad."[25]

Apparently tithing was gaining momentum in the denomination by 1964. The House of Bishops concurred with another resolution urging "all members of the Church to practice tithing."[26] In 1982, the Convention affirmed the tithe as "the minimum standard of giving for Episcopalians."[27] They added: "We Deputies and Bishops do hereby pledge ourselves to tithe, or to work towards tithing, as a minimum standard of our own giving and of our witness in the world."[28] With these words, they seemed to affirm

21 From *The Book of Discipline of The United Methodist Church—1988*. Copyright © 1988 by The United Methodist Publishing House. Used by permission; page 161.

22 From *The Book of Discipline of The United Methodist Church—1988*; page 376. (When all descriptions of local-church and conference organization were eliminated from the *Discipline* by the 1996 General Conference, these two sections were eliminated by default.)

23 *The Book of Resolutions of The United Methodist Church—1996* (The United Methodist Publishing House, 1996); pages 715–716.

24 From *Journal of the General Convention of the Protestant Episcopal Church in the United States of America, 1940*; page 152.

25 From *Journal of the General Convention of the Protestant Episcopal Church in the United States of America, 1955*; page 254.

26 From *Journal of the General Convention of the Protestant Episcopal Church in the United States of America, 1964*; page 356.

27 From *Journal of the General Convention of . . . The Episcopal Church, 1982* (New York: General Convention, 1983); page C-111.

28 From *Journal of the General Convention of . . . The Episcopal Church, 1982* (New York: General Convention, 1983); page C-111.

tithing as a benchmark to work toward as well as a fixed norm. The tithe is also recognized as a Christian witness (although they did not elaborate on this concept).

Peer pressure was added in a 1997 General Convention resolution. The resolution asked for all deputies and bishops of the Convention to sign a commitment to tithing, and for the signatures to be published in their *Journal*.[29]

Denominational statements are not a panacea. Some tithers separate themselves from God and depend upon their keeping the law rather than upon experiencing the grace of a loving God for their salvation. However, just because some people take a good thing and use it in a bad way is no reason to toss out the whole concept. For many of us, excessive attention to our possessions is keeping us from an intimate relationship with God. Tithing is a discipline that pares away at our obsession with things and frees us for a closer relationship with God.

Tithing has a rich heritage in the Christian faith and in the traditions of the early church. We appeal for the discipline of tithing to be renewed in the present and the future. If we do not once again learn to send the holy smoke of that which we value up to the Lord who made it all, we may soon find ourselves with little of real value left.

Tithing is an intentional act that reminds us of our connection with God. When we are connected with God, we see a different set of values than those urged upon us by the culture of the time. Therefore, tithing is an act that recognizes, first, that the "stuff" we accumulate does not bring happiness, and, second, that a relationship with God and God's creation is an enduring value.

---

29 *Journal of the General Convention of . . . The Episcopal Church, 1997*; resolution A138s.

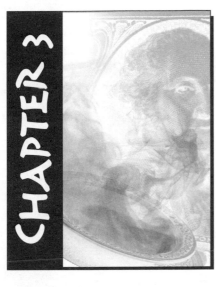

CHAPTER 3

Holy $moke Is Valid:
The Fat Still Belongs to God

Then the priest shall turn these into smoke on the altar as a food offering by fire for a pleasing odor. All fat is the LORD's.

(Leviticus 3:16)

Each of you must give as you have made up your mind, not reluctantly or under compulsion, for God loves a cheerful giver.

(2 Corinthians 9:7)

Every preacher has heard the comment following the Sunday sermon: "Well, Reverend, that all sounded just fine. But what does that have to do with us?" All good sermons should quickly apply the Scripture to the people, for their time.

In the previous two chapters, we have tried to lay a historical, scriptural, and theological foundation for making holy smoke in the twenty-first century. This chapter applies this previous discussion to the questions about tithing and giving that people in the pews are asking today, and will likely continue to ask in the next millennium.

Is the Tithe Legalism?

"Jesus calls us to be disciples. But I do not see where he ever called us to be tithers. Oh, according to the Gospel of Matthew, Jesus mentioned the word; but the authenticity of that passage is a bit suspect. Jesus wants much more than a tithe. He wants disciples, not dollar bills. I don't see that preaching and teaching on tithing is even healthy for the Christian today. I sure don't want to get caught up in that kind of old-fashioned legalism. I am going to call on people to give all of their lives to Christ."

This statement is a compilation of what many people have told us when we asked about the practice of tithing in their congregations. These people assert that tithing conflicts with grace, and they don't want to go back to law. They find tithing hard to define in the modern world. They don't know how to calculate the tithe in relation to paying Social Security taxes, income taxes, deferred pension plans, housing allowances, and so forth.

We acknowledge that tithing isn't mathematically simple. And yet, the fat belongs to the Lord! But today the fat is in our wallets and bank accounts. Many of us don't feel affluent. Indeed, the bills are as great as the income. We complain about not having *any* fat. In fact, to hear the way many of us talk, one would think that the lean is getting pared away.

We cannot find any place in the Bible that says that tithing is a universal law. There are times and places in the Scriptures where people are shamed, scolded, and even berated for not tithing; but there is no record of punishment to those who fail to follow through. Grace reigns! Or, conversely, we could say that sin continues. The tithe does, however, appear to be a benchmark prescribed for individuals and nations to assess their relationship with God and with the space God occupies in their lives. Unfortunately, there is no consistent biblical formula to follow. Even in the days when the new nation was formed in the Promised Land, there were taxes. These varied from age to age, depending upon which government was in power in Israel. If the tax was ten percent, it was called a tithe.

In the religious community, the decision to tithe was a free choice on the part of the Israelite giver; it was never compelled. The tithe was meant to be something of value given out of one's relationship with God. Wherever the relationship was healthy, the tithe was given first—off the top. Paying the tithe first was a sign of the donor's (tenant, steward, landowner) priorities. The tithe was pleasing to God when it witnessed to a relationship with God. But the tithe was an offense to God whenever it was given in an attempt to bargain with or manipulate the Creator.

Today we don't calibrate our income in cattle and sheep. Our measurements are dollars and cents. Even for us modern-day people, the tithe is a valid discipline to teach and to practice, for the same reasons holy smoke was offered by the early Hebrews. To be sure, God doesn't need one tenth; God calls us to use one hundred percent for the good of the world. Yet we need to offer gifts to the Creator so that God might transform the gifts; the needs of the world depend upon it! What's more, the portion of the one hundred percent that we offer is given to sanctify the whole. The giver needs to give it!

Many leaders are uncomfortable with (or opposed to) recommending the tithe as a benchmark for giving today. Tithing has been used as a club—a piece of legalism—with which to spiritually coerce people into propping up church budgets. But just because a good thing has been abused doesn't mean that it needs to be tossed out. We are making an appeal for a fresh look at this ancient practice.

Tithing has been called an Old Testament law that is superseded by New Testament grace. One of the most "noble" ways to avoid the issue of tithing is to appeal to the witness (or silence) of the New Testament with regard to tithing. Because the Gospels have few references and Paul is silent on the subject of tithing, some people argue that Christians today should also be silent about the practice. However, the Scriptures are silent about a variety of things that many Christians today hold to be important to the witness of the faith. For instance, many church leaders who make the argument against tithing based on the silence of the New Testament are often the same ones who urge Christians to march in a civil-rights rally. They implore people to attend worship and Sunday school regularly. They advocate working in a soup kitchen, writing letters to oppose abortions, or going on work camps to Mexico or Russia. They promote advocacy to halt the sale of pornographic books—the list goes on. But the fact is, not one of these items is explicitly named in the New Testament.

In other words, guidelines or benchmarks are presumed to be appropriate for correct spiritual behavior in almost all areas of life, except finance. In fact, a person's spiritual progress and gifts are often judged based on the priorities of the person doing the judging. We can't have it both ways.

As good as it sounds, we do not agree that either the absence of any direct commandment in the New Testament to tithe, or the fear of legalism, are valid reasons for abstaining from recommending tithing as a spiritual discipline in the twenty-first century.

Dietrich Bonhoeffer helpfully described both legalism and grace. In his book *The Cost of Discipleship*, the German Christian martyr paints a vivid contrast between "costly grace" and "cheap grace." Cheap grace means to accept the sacrifice of Christ, assuming that it costs us nothing when it is given and costs us nothing to make use of today. In other words, cheap grace is a one-way street placing no responsibility upon the recipients of grace. Accepting responsibility is not the same as legalism.[1]

For us, Bonhoeffer seems to use the image of parental grace as a description of costly grace. A good parent freely gives love to the child even when the love is undeserved. However, the ever-present hope of the giver (the parent) is that the recipient will grow into a sense of responsibility and respond to that love in many positive ways.

The child who refuses to express appreciation and adoration to loving parents who selflessly gave themselves to him or her for twenty years would be considered selfish, rude, immature, or worse. Returning love in response to love is one sign of a mature person. Responding to a spouse for grace received is an important ingredient for growing a healthy marriage. Learning to give unto God through the benchmark of tithing is a way to mature as a Christian and grow into spiritual adulthood. Such action has nothing to do with legalism and everything to do with grace—costly grace!

---

1 For Bonhoeffer's discussion of "cheap" and "costly" grace, see *The Cost of Discipleship* (The MacMillan Company, 1959).

The present generation did not invent opposition to tithing. The tithe was often misunderstood in biblical times. Ever since then, it has been both understood and misunderstood. The discipline of tithing is not meant to be law. There has been no punishment on the individual for failing to do it.[2] Without a set of consequences for disobedience, tithing cannot be a law. It was, and we believe should still be, an encouraging guide or benchmark for sound healthy living. Like other good things, tithing can be distorted. However, we contend that tithing is just as helpful a benchmark for giving today as it was in the past.

If Their Hearts Are Right, Won't the Money Come?

"Why do you talk about tithing? I believe that if people just got their hearts right with God, the church would have plenty of money. Tithing is not the issue. We need to work on the soul."

This statement is *almost* correct. When we urge tithing, we hope that people will hear that we are talking more about conversion than about money. The goal of the Christian faith is not to get everyone to tithe. The aim is to further the reign of God on earth. We believe that tithing is both a sign of God's reign within the individual and an instrument that God uses to enlarge the Kingdom. In other words, tithing *is* working on the soul; but it is also working on the whole person—body, mind, and spirit.

There is another aspect of the statement that bothers us. It sounds like the whole point of getting people to tithe is to ensure that the church will have plenty of money. The truth is, it is more important for the church to have a mission than for it to have money. Money without a God-given mission is destructive. Nevertheless, mission without money is impossible.

The personal dimension of tithing cannot be separated from the institutional mission, but the two are distinct. People need to give for their souls' sake *as well as* for the good that their tithes do for others. Holy smoke is the benchmark to help the individual giver put his or her financial life in order. Jesus was greatly concerned about the wealthy whose hearts were ruled far more by their possessions than by God. The tithe played a significant role in helping "a camel to go through the eye of a needle" (Matthew 19:24). The heart was always the issue. The tithe can help lead the heart to God, and once there can maintain the relationship.

---

2 We acknowledge that Malachi 3:6-12 seems to indicate that failure to tithe has consequences for the nation. However, the lack of tithing is a symbol of a broken relationship. Thus, when the *relationship* between God and Israel is damaged, dire consequences result for the nation. See pages 25–26 for our commentary on Malachi.

Is Social Security a Part of My Tithe?

"But wait a minute. The Hebrews didn't have Social Security, and the government didn't have a welfare program like we have in America to take care of widows, orphans, poor people, and sick people. I pay my taxes right on schedule, and they are considerably more than the ten percent tithe you talked about. I think paying these taxes is enough! I am doing my part in giving when I write my check to Uncle Sam on April 15. Times have changed, and so should the instruction for the tithe. Why, I bet if Jesus were here today, he would talk about the need for more welfare programs and food aid rather than about tithing."

Tithing was never a part of the religious life of God's people because God needed more fat cows or more dollar bills. Tithing was not developed as a part of the religious life of ancient nations so that the religious institution could prosper. Historically, at its best tithing has been a benchmark for spirituality.

Tithing is both a sign and a means. It is a sign of a relationship between the giver and God. Taxes can never fill that need. Many tithers can testify that the discipline of tithing has helped them grow more into the likeness of the Creator and has helped them be less inclined to worship themselves or other idols. To be sure, tithes were brought to the storehouse and given out to the needy; but the ones who gained the most from tithing were the donors.

Paul urged the Corinthians to give cheerfully, not reluctantly or under compulsion (2 Corinthians 9:6-7). Social Security and income taxes are not choices for most of us. The laws of the land compel us to pay taxes, and most of us do it with considerable reluctance—without even a smile on our faces. Paul calls for "hilarious" givers! We are so bold as to believe that tithing can bring joy back to the act of giving. We will not claim that paying taxes will bring great joy!

The church can use a dollar given reluctantly just as easily as it can a dollar given cheerfully. Unfortunately, the reluctant giver receives no blessing from the act of giving. God is as concerned with the heart of the giver giving the gift as with the institution (church) receiving it. The secret to God's reign is to change the hearts of men and women, not to build up big bank accounts in a religious institution. When the government is the only route for reaching out to others, then the members of the society fail to grow in the spiritual power necessary to make a real difference in the world.

Offering up the holy smoke of the tithe as a spiritual discipline can build the spiritual muscle necessary to change lives and to make disciples. Taxes and Social Security are no more of a gift to God than paying dues at a health club is the way to a stronger body. Unless one voluntarily chooses to participate in a fitness program, he or she will remain just as unhealthy and just as flabby. Unless a person learns to give cheerfully through spiritual discipline, he or she will remain a spiritual potbelly. Paying taxes won't cut it.

Considering the fact that the members of Christian churches today give an average of slightly more than two percent of their incomes, let's reflect on what would happen if half of all church members tithed. We probably wouldn't need Social Security or welfare in anywhere near their present forms. Income to churches would rise from $70 billion (in 1996) to $125 billion. Theoretically (even assuming that churches will take care of administration and maintenance needs first), most of the additional $55 billion could be used for missional giving such as care of the elderly, the hungry, and the poor.

A relationship with God has at least three dimensions: God, the self, and others. All three dimensions are important. Who can forget the forceful passage of Matthew 25:31-46, in which Jesus said, "Just as you did it to one of the least of these who are members of my family, you did it to me"? The church in contemporary culture can't do it all; however, we *are* called to do something! The attempt to place all the responsibility on the government is an abdication of our call as Christian givers. It is a sign of selfishness. It is unhealthy and will make us "fat."

$hould the Whole Tithe Go to the Church?

> *"I give my money in lots of places. The soup kitchen at the local mission is a favorite charity of mine. I also give to the Cancer Society and to the Heart Fund. I count these in my tithe. These institutions do good work. They are helping God's children even if they aren't doing a lot of preaching and converting. It is still good work, and I think God would want me to help them out."*

This argument is a good one. Apparently the soup kitchen of ancient Israel was the synagogue. In the time of the Acts of the Apostles, the early church was responsible for feeding the widows and others in need (Acts 6:1-6). If they didn't do it, it wouldn't get done.

Malachi called on the Israelites to deliver the tithes to the storehouse (Malachi 3:6-12). This storehouse was a series of rooms attached to the Temple, where the tithes of grain, oil, wine, and livestock were brought. The storehouse was also a distribution center.

Records indicate that the supplies in the storehouse were dispensed in three ways. One part went to the tribe of Levi. (See Numbers 18.) This is similar to paying the pastor and other church staff who operate as overseers of the storehouse. A second amount went to orphans and widows. These people were powerless in biblical society unless cared for through the store-house or by extended family. We might compare this to the "safety net" concept of modern welfare assistance. The third portion went to Gentile poor. Today we would view these people as the unchurched—those outside the community of faith.

Some Christian leaders assert that the storehouse in our society is the church and thus should receive the entire tithe. We are not ready to make that judgment—we wish we could. Far too many churches are doing noth-ing more than maintaining old buildings and propping up the institution. The eyes of these churches have turned inward. They have neither the vision of Christ nor the heart of Christ. They exist to serve themselves. We are hard-pressed to argue that God wants tithes to be brought to such a body. Simply having the name *church* on the front-lawn sign does not justify receiving a tithe from anyone. Propping up a selfish church is similar to supporting the synagogue like the Pharisees did, while they overlooked weightier matters like justice and love of God.

The giver has a significant responsibility to use prayerful judgment in giving any gift. If a church is one in name only, then it needs to repent and walk in a new direction. Such a church and those who help it stay that way are under the judgment of God. However, we need to be careful about trying to take the judgment of God into our own hands. Do not jump to judgment!

We urge tithers who are concerned about the way their congregation spends money to visit with the pastor and lay leadership. It is proper to raise questions about how the tithes are used. Share your vision of the con-gregation's future. With the pastor and other leaders, prayerfully explore what it would mean for the congregation if the number of tithers grew dra-matically. Discernment about disbursing the overflow from the storehouse may lead to a fresh look at the vision. It may even lead the way to renewal of the church.

Tithers have no more and no less right to share their insights into how the Spirit is leading the church to use its gifts. Each of us has been given a measure of influence. It is our responsibility as stewards to participate in spiritually discerning how funds should be allocated. In fact, not to do so is failing to use all of our God-given talent.

Many churches today could and would be the "storehouse" for missional distribution if supported more generously by the membership. The failings of the church to reach out beyond itself may not be the fault of the pastoral and lay leadership but of the flock, who prefer to be fed by the church rather than to help "feed my sheep." (See John 21:15-17.) It takes the lead-ership and the followership working together and giving together to truly resemble the missional body of Christ.

This is a two-dimensional call. First, it is a call for congregations to examine their spending (distribution) decisions. Second, we urge growing Christians to work toward the tithe (tenth part) as a benchmark. Then we propose that the tithe be given through this latter-day storehouse. Funds over and above the tithe (as one is able to give them) may go to other worthwhile causes. The church has a mission and the opportunity to trans-form the world. Therefore, we advocate supporting the church first and foremost through the spiritual discipline of tithing, as long as the congregation is struggling to faithfully fulfill its mission in the world.

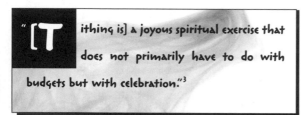

" [T ithing is] a joyous spiritual exercise that does not primarily have to do with budgets but with celebration."[3]

We recognize the importance of integrity and trust when it comes to giving. In large churches and in small chapels, there are people who tithe and who are troubled by the poor stewardship of their congregations. No church (congregation or denomination) perfectly fulfills Christ's call on its life. These institutions are no more perfect than their leaders and members. In the end, each of us must give as he or she feels led by the Holy Spirit and not as dictated by a self that seeks to control. Not giving at all, it needs to be pointed out, is the worst option and the most spiritually damaging. Make holy smoke!

How Do I Figure the Tenth?

"Well, if I am going to tithe, how do I figure one tenth of my income? Is it one tenth of the gross income or one tenth of the net income? In Abraham's time, it was a lot easier to figure out the tenth than it is now. If you had ten bushels of grain, one bushel went to the Lord; if you had ten sheep, one was sacrificed. There are so many deductions on my check that I can't even name them all. After they take money out for pension; health insurance; life insurance; city, state, and federal taxes; the office charity fund; and a bunch of other stuff, there isn't much left. How much does my benchmark amount to on this tithing venture?"

Our first reaction to this comment is to be thankful that this person wants to go as far as to figure out the tithe. We estimate that fewer than five percent of church members tithe, and even fewer in the congregations of "traditional" (mainline) denominations. We rejoice whenever we hear of a church member wanting to engage in the spiritual discipline of tithing.

3 From *Congregations at the Crossroads: Remembering to Be Households of God*, by Ronald E. Vallet (William B. Eerdmans Publishing Company, 1998); page123. Used by permission.

Historical and biblical records indicate that tithing started out relating only to crops. Later on, animals also were included. We live in a different economic system today than the Hebrews did thousands of years ago. Our task is to discover the underlying principles and relationships with regard to tithing rather than the literal formulas.

The starting point is the relationship between God and God's people. Tithing is not a fundraising practice but a devotional sign of a growing relationship between the human creature and the Creator. It is a response to what God has done and an anticipation of God's continuing care and love. The question is, What is an appropriate sign to show my response of gratitude? The accumulation of biblical witness, tradition, and human experience points to the tithe as such a sign or benchmark.

"Do not you know that God entrusted you with that money (all above what buys necessaries for your families) to feed the hungry, to clothe the naked, to help the stranger, the widow, the fatherless; and, indeed, as far as it will go, to relieve the wants of all mankind? How can you, how dare you, defraud your Lord, by applying it to any other purpose?" [4]

We recognize that we have still not provided a formula for figuring any individual's or family's tithe. Here is our starting point: *The tithe is figured on the portion of resources over which we have a choice.*

Tithing is a decision. You have no choice in how much tax you will pay once the law of the land is enacted. On the other hand, many of us have great latitude over how much money will go into a 401k or a 403b retirement plan account. Include the amounts you voluntarily choose to send away prior to receiving your income.

Second, review your expenses. Many people claim that tithing is not possible because less than one or two percent is left over after taking care of all obligations. That is a clear call to examine the obligations in light of one's values. Mortgages, car payments, eating out, golf, expensive vacations, private schools, and credit card bills all become obligations. The question must be asked, "What holds the highest priority for me?" One cannot serve two masters, Jesus said. Each of us has to choose whether we are going to serve at the foot of the Almighty Dollar or at the foot of the Almighty God.

The benchmark of tithing helps reestablish appropriate priorities in life. When the golden calf looks too good, the soul is in jeopardy. Tithing is a

4 From "On the Danger of Increasing Riches," by John Wesley, in *The Works of John Wesley*, Volume Seven; page 360.

helpful discipline to call people back to fiscal sanity. The tithe is never an excuse for recklessly spending the other ninety percent. Unless tithing helps put the whole of our economic life in order, it is merely sounding brass and noisy cymbals. The mortgage, car payment, vacation, and "new toy" are decisions made either under the lordship of Christ or the lordship of the devil. Every place where money is spent and invested is a matter of justice and righteousness for the child of God.

What expenditures help my relationships with God and with others? What expenses get in the way of these relationships? It's as simple as that. Many of us need a trusted friend who is willing to listen to us as we try to sort out the important from the less important in our lives.

Simplicity is needed—especially for new tithers. Let us suggest the following formula: If you are able to deposit one thousand dollars of your paycheck into your account, then a tithe is one hundred dollars. A tither will systematically, and with discipline, set aside the first hundred dollars as the tithe. The remaining nine hundred dollars is used in ways that would not bring embarrassment when standing before the Lord. This simple formula will at least help get one started with tithing as the benchmark.

Many people feel that they are not able to start out at ten percent because of decisions made prior to the choice to tithe. It is important to establish a plan to work toward the benchmark of tithing.

Arriving at giving ten percent of one's income is not the end of the spiritual race. The tithe is a benchmark, not the final goal. John Wesley urged his followers to calculate their giving on a different basis from the tithe.[5] He advocated a careful examination of how much money a person needed to live on. He did not confuse needs with wants. Live as frugally as you can, Wesley said. Spend for the necessities and give all the rest away. For Wesley, a fixed percentage was irrelevant.

Many people need to move far beyond giving ten percent. A wealthy giver may hardly notice the biblical tithe. The tithe is a benchmark along the way. After reaching the benchmark, one should set a new one. Remember that *all* the fat belongs to the Lord.

Does the Tithe Include Time as well as Finances?

> "I cannot give money to my church, but I try to make up for it by giving my time."

We want to commend all those who wrestle with the issue of giving of one's time as well as one's money. All of us have heard the statement that

---

5 In his sermon "The Use of Money," Wesley counsels his parishioners to gain all they can, to save all they can, and to give all they can. (*The Works of John Wesley*, Volume Six; pages 124–136.) By *save,* Wesley meant refraining from purchasing anything that was not a necessity. He did not consider saving to mean putting money away for a rainy day, or for an expensive vacation.

"time is money." Volunteering time through the ministry of the church is important. All studies of giving in America indicate that the people who give the most money are also the ones who give the most time. This connection between time and money is accurate for charitable non-profit organizations as well as for churches.

However, the statement, "I cannot give money to my church, but I try to make up for it by giving my time," is also disturbing; for it sounds like the person is trying to work out a deal with God rather than to offer a gift of love. The attitude behind the statement surely doesn't resemble that of the poor widow who placed her last two coins in the Temple offering box and was blessed for it. Jesus did not say that she should have substituted her time for the money. He also didn't say that it was the monetary value of her gift that merited the blessing.

The widow's blessing came before, during, and after the gift, because she truly had the love of God in her heart. We can only speculate, but we doubt that this woman lost sleep over priorities. She obviously had a deep and abiding relationship with God. She knew who she was and who she wasn't. Hers was a fulfilled life.

In establishing tithing as a benchmark for giving, we fully acknowledge that there are no set measurements to calculate spiritual health. We recognize our own need for yardsticks and believe that they are helpful for all people seeking to grow in their discipleship.

The answer to the question about time is, Time should be included in our response to God, because all of life is included under the lordship of Christ. God wants one hundred percent of our lives, and we are called to ever strive to give God that.

Setting up ten percent of our income as a benchmark is a bit easier to establish and measure than ten percent of our time. For example, is attending worship a part of the ten percent? Did I use the service last Sunday to enhance business contacts instead of worshiping God? Does sleeping count in tabulating total hours, or do only the hours when I'm awake count? Is coaching a Little League team the same as going on a mission trip to Mexico?

It concerns us when church leaders include only time spent in the institutional church as time given to God. The layperson's primary ministry is in the world. The time spent within the church has the same symbolic value as paying the tithe. However, devoting ten percent of our time to the church's ministry does not amount to a bargain with God so that we can spend the rest of the time doing things *we* want to do. "Tithing" our time is a commitment to grow so that all we do with our time is what both God and we want.

Although it won't be easy, we encourage people to establish benchmarks for time and talent, just as they do for finances. The question is never time *versus* finances or time *versus* talent; after all, all of our lives belong to God.

One cannot substitute one for the other and contribute to spiritual growth in the same way.

If Tithing Is a Benchmark, How Do I Know When I Have Reached the Pinnacle?

"If I start out along the path of tithing, when will I know that I have made it? Is establishing a benchmark some kind of trick to get me to start giving at ten percent, only to then be expected to give fifteen percent or even twenty percent? I know when I will have my house paid off. How will I know when I have given enough?"

We imagine that there were times during Jesus' moments of solitude in the desert that he prayed to the Father: "I have taught in just about every town in this area. Is that enough? I have healed hundreds of people. Is that enough? I have recruited several assistants for the work of the Kingdom; many others are following along. Is that enough? I have fed thousands. Is that enough?" We think we know the answer to those imaginary prayers. Jesus pled for the cup to be taken away, and the Father said, "I have a plan for your life, and that plan means that you still have a cross in your future." Jesus obediently said, "Not my will but yours be done." (See Luke 22:39-42.)

Jesus' response to his Father is the Christian's best example of giving. Giving to God does not consist of a set of boxes one can check, with categories like "tithe," "missionary service," and "next-door neighbor." We could never set an objective standard that, when we reach it, will prompt God to say, "Enough." God isn't finished with our lives. We are all "Christians under construction." We can be sure that God's work in our lives is not finished yet.

The purpose of rendering holy smoke through the regular discipline of tithing is to help us stay healthy enough spiritually so that we may be able to hear what the Lord ultimately wants from our whole lives. Am I in the place where I'm supposed to be? Is there a cross in my future? The ultimate question to God is not how much we want to give but how God wants us to live. The discipline of tithing helps us reflect on the most faithful way to use the remaining ninety percent of our income, which, as we have said several times now, also belongs to God.

The following is a practical example of the tithe functioning as a benchmark rather than as a goal or a pinnacle. The first benchmark a pastor we know set was to tithe on the adjusted net income. In other words, the tithe did not include the value of the parsonage. The pastor then set a new benchmark—tithing on gross income, including the housing allowance. Now another benchmark has been set. After this benchmark is reached, the pastor will continue to set new benchmarks.

John Wesley taught the principle that Christians are always going on to perfection. They may never reach perfection in *this* life. And if perfection does come, it is a gift of grace rather than an achievement. Jesus has already reached out to us in grace, saying, "Come to me." We don't have to tithe or to do anything else to come to Jesus. However, once we have accepted Jesus' invitation to discipleship and have affirmed the relationship, we

"The generality of Christians usually set apart something yearly, perhaps a tenth or even one-eighth part of their income, whether it arise from yearly revenue, or from trade, for charitable uses. A few I have known, who said, like Zaccheus [sic], 'Lord, the half of my goods I give to the poor.' O that it would please God to multiply those friends of mankind, those general benefactors!" [6]

want to do things to witness to the connection. We want to do those things that get the response, "Well done, good and faithful servant" (Matthew 25:21, adapted).

If we are looking for a level of giving where we can pat ourselves on the back and feel that we have completed our obligations to Christ for his death and sacrifice, then we have totally missed the boat. Only God has the power to say "enough." On the other hand, we don't have to feel guilty about not reaching perfection. God's grace allows us to enjoy the journey of discipleship rather than feeling condemned about not getting to the finish line.

Yes, we believe that the tithe is appropriate today—even in this modern economy. We offer the tithe to God in the hope that it is both a witness of our relationship to Christ and a discipline through which to develop an openness to a more wholesome relationship with him. Tithing is a great place to start our response of gratitude for God's grace.

6 From "The More Excellent Way," by John Wesley, in *The Works of John Wesley*, Volume Seven; pages 35–36.

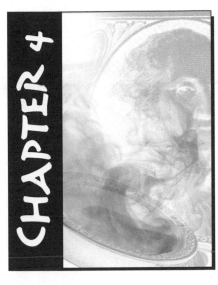

CHAPTER 4

Holy $moke in Your Congregation:
A Process for Inviting Pilgrims Into the Adventure of Tithing

How do you get from where you are to where you want to be? Moving from one level of giving to another is a pilgrimage. It's an adventure. Like travel, it opens up new worlds and changes perspectives on life. As kids would say about something truly exciting, "It's awesome." We invite you to take this awesome journey into tithing as part of your walk with Christ.

Every journey needs a road map. The map outlined in this chapter guides a small group of people on one segment of the adventure of Christian living: tithing. Tithing is not the whole of the life of faith;

Is not this the fast that I choose:

to loose the bonds of injustice,

to undo the thongs of the yoke,

to let the oppressed go free,

and to break every yoke?

Is it not to share your bread with the hungry,

and bring the homeless poor into your house?

(Isaiah 58:6-7a)

nor is it proof that a person is a follower of Jesus. Tithing is a discipline of the spiritual life. We dare to claim it is both a response to grace and a means of grace.

A means of grace is an action or rite whereby God's presence and love are experienced. Some means of grace, such as the sacraments of baptism and Eucharist, are commonly practiced in the church. Others are more occasional. John Wesley urged followers of Christ to avail themselves of the means of grace in their movement toward perfection. His list of the means of grace includes the sacraments, prayer, and Bible study.

Wesley also named fasting as a means of grace. For some people, tithing is an act of financial fasting. It is an intentional action to focus attention away from the lesser and toward the greater. This is exactly what was behind the Hebrew tradition of offering up holy smoke.

Holy smoke, like tithing, was intended as a sacrifice. It was an action of setting aside something specific. Unfortunately, sacrifice has become a "heavy" word today. When most of us hear the word *sacrifice*, we think of the agony of giving up something rather than of the benefits resulting from the action.

Fasting from certain kinds of foods yields both spiritual and physical good. For instance, abstaining from eating chocolate during Lent may be a kindly act to one's body. If I like chocolate, the craving reminds me why I decided to give up this snack during the Lenten season. In that sense, tithing is symbolic; it points beyond itself to the reality of Christ's sacrificial suffering and death.

In addition to the spiritual prompting that fasting provides, opportunities also come to be a witness to others. One may respond this way to an offer: "No, thank you. I have given up chocolate for Lent." Such a statement may present an opportunity to witness to others about the why of fasting.

In the same way, tithing—or financial fasting—is an act of setting aside some of our financial resources so that we can focus our attention on the spiritual rather than on the material—on the Creator rather than on created things. Financial fasting is an act to help us "get our act together." Although financial fasting is a witness, it is done not for show but for sharing in the mind and heart of God.

However, tithing is no more "rational" than fasting. Indeed, our North American culture affirms neither tithing nor fasting. Popular movies, television advertisements, and the air we breathe seem to extol accumulating stuff—the bigger, the better; the more, the merrier. Honors go to the Bill Gateses and Ted Turners of the world. The spiritual discipline of tithing appeals to a different standard. Even though the benefits are great, living in contrast with the prevailing culture requires all the help we can get.

For this reason, we believe that people need the support of a community—a group of fellow pilgrims—along the journey towards tithing. People need reminders from one another that happiness is not the product of bigger paychecks and fancier houses. When the tithes of our Hebrew ancestors were brought into the Temple, the Hebrews held a big celebration. No biblical story urges secret, individualistic tithing practices. Tithing was an act of public worship and festivity. Making holy smoke was a time of eating, drinking, and dancing with friends.

Our Hebrew forebears told stories. Like the sacrifices and tithes of their time, so the tithe today is an instrument to help us remember our story as God's people. Whose are we? Why are we here? The paraphrase of Deuteronomy 14:23c in *The Living Bible* says that God gave us the tithe so that in every aspect in our lives we might "put God first."[1] As part of God's family, we have a story. We have a history. A story always suggests a communal context; it is never an isolated act of the individual.

Therefore, in the process toward tithing described in this chapter, we urge that the journey be undertaken in community—with a group of fellow travelers. Encourage one another along the way. Weep with those who weep and laugh with those who laugh. Help one another move beyond the starting point to a deeper level of relationship with God and with God's creation. Let the tithe be the symbol of that growth. We invite you to see what *holy smoke* can mean in your relationship with God, family, and friends, and in the community around you. Let the journey begin.

Journey Into Tithing: An Outline of the Process

In what follows, we describe a process for guiding a group of people in the congregation who wish to learn how to practice the discipline of tithing. The process involves a carefully selected group of people who will journey together for a period from as brief as thirty days to as long as six-and-a-half months, depending on the individual's choice. However, each person must commit (by signing a covenant) to at least the initial thirty-day experience.

At the end of the initial thirty-day experience, members of the core group are given the opportunity to continue the journey into tithing for another ten weeks. Upon completion of the ten-week period, group members have the opportunity to enter the final phase of the process by committing to meet on a monthly basis for another three months.

The recommended schedule follows:

July through August: Planning, preparation, and recruitment of core group
September: Thirty-day initial journey of meditation and prayer
October through November: Ten-week extension
Mid-January through mid-April: Three-month continuation of the journey

1 Taken from *The Living Bible*, copyright © 1971. Used by permission of Tyndale House Publishers, Wheaton, Illinois 60189. All rights reserved.

When	Who	What
July–August	Small planning group (Leadership team)	Planning Preparation Recruiting of core group
September	Core group	Thirty-day journey
October–November	Core group members who choose to continue the journey	Ten-week journey
December	The whole church	Celebrate Advent/ Christmas
January–March or February–April	Core-group members who choose to continue the journey	Three-month continuation of the spiritual journey
April or May	Leadership group	Assess the experience with the core group
June	Leadership group	Plan for the next cycle

$electing the Core Group

Begin with a pilot core group. We recommend that the initial group be carefully selected and their participation be solicited by personal invitation. Select people who are leaders or potential leaders in the congregation. An ideal size for the pilot group is eight to twelve people.

Especially consider people who have completed the DISCIPLE Bible study, the Walk to Emmaus, or another significant spiritual-growth experience. The lead group also may be the Committee of Finance, although we rarely recommend it. In most congregations, choosing people by office is rarely the best means of selecting a core group.

The church council (or another administrative group) can become a second group to undertake the process, after the initial group has had a chance to complete the journey toward tithing. In most churches the governing board is too large a group and may not constitute core leadership for the future. Above all, do not issue broadside invitations for "whosoever will may come."

It is appropriate for the core group to include people who already tithe, as long as they are open to growing in their pilgrimage of giving. Remember, the tithe is a benchmark rather than a destination!

When issuing the invitation to individuals to join the core group, clearly state the contents of the covenant:

- Each person is asked to commit to a thirty-day experiment, with daily reflection on the recommended Scripture passages, as well as daily prayer.
- Each person will participate in four sessions with the core group, one session per week.
- Each person is to pray for each member of the core group by name each day.
- Each person will study HOLY SMOKE: WHATEVER HAPPENED TO TITHING? with the group as recommended.
- At the end of the thirty days, each group member will write a "contract" outlining his or her next steps on the spiritual journey.

Meetings of Core Group

Time, Place, and Leadership

The core group gathers each week for ninety minutes, at a time that works best for the participants. The meeting room can be in a home or at the church. The room should be amenable to discussion, prayer, and reflection. It is appropriate to provide coffee, tea, or soft drinks for the group, but not food. The quantity and "fanciness" of the food tends to escalate from week to week.

Hold an orientation meeting for the group a week before the first session. The pastor should conduct the orientation session. Often the pastor will continue as the leader of the weekly meetings. The leader must be willing to lead by listening rather than by talking.

At the orientation meeting, present a copy of HOLY SMOKE! to each participant. Referring to Appendix I, "Scripture Readings for Each Day of the Thirty-Day Experiment," describe how the designated texts are used for individual study. The initial group of eight to twelve people will make a commitment to study the biblical passages and readings from HOLY SMOKE! on a weekly basis. The group will meet once a week to allow participants to discuss their experience with the journey toward tithing. Be sure to clarify the time and place for these weekly meetings. Other small groups may follow the process after the core group has finished its thirty-day experiment.

The leader will refer to the text of HOLY SMOKE! in each week's session, with the assumption that everyone has read the assigned material. The assigned reading from the chapters is noted in Appendix I.

As leader, explain the entire six-and-a-half-month process and make sure everyone understands what is involved. Also emphasize that anyone can drop out after the initial thirty-day period with no prejudice.

Format for Each Session

We recommend the following format for structuring the four weekly group meetings.

Centering Time (10 minutes)

Begin each session with a time of centering. During this time of quiet, participants seek to be present with one another and with God. Ask for prayer concerns, including upcoming events in the life of a participant—a trip, a job interview—that he or she wants the group to remember in prayer. As leader, plan this time with sensitivity to needs. End the time with a spoken prayer.

Sharing Joys and Struggles (35 minutes)

Let each person share an insight, experience, struggle, or question arising from reading the assigned Bible passages, or from meditation and action undertaken during the week. Ask: "What did God say to you this week? Where is the Spirit nudging you to go?"

As leader, be careful about giving advice. This is a time for participants to share and to encourage one another. Each individual has to address his or her own problems. Participants need encouragement and support, not careless solutions. Help the group assess what each person wants or needs from the group.

Discussion of HOLY SMOKE! (30 minutes)

Lead the group members in a discussion of their reflections on the assigned pages from HOLY SMOKE! Be sure to include in the discussion the review questions on the book. These appear with the Scripture reading for days 7, 14, 21, and 30.

Requests for Prayer Support (10 minutes)

Invite each person to write down on a slip of paper one item (or area of discipleship) for which he or she would like the other members of the group to pray in the week ahead. Have participants put their names on the strips of paper. Place the pieces of paper in the center of the room and ask participants to take a fellow member's prayer request.

Closing (5 minutes)

Offer a closing prayer or invite anyone who wishes to offer a brief prayer. It is appropriate for the group members to hold hands during prayer as a way to symbolize their connection as a body of fellow pilgrims.

Service of Dedication for the Core Group

The following litany can be used during a regular service of worship in the church. Worship leaders will find an appropriate time during the service to commission the core group for the adventure in tithing.

Invite the members of the core group to gather at the front of the congregation. The pastor says to the congregation:
Brothers and sisters, from time to time we provide opportunities for people to come together to explore new ways to help make the connections between faith and daily life. A particularly difficult connection to make in our culture is the one between faith and money. The group of people here before you have expressed a willingness to be open to God through the reading of Scripture, prayer, and study together over the next month to explore God's will in relation to their giving.

The pastor addresses the core group:
During the next thirty days you will be engaged in an exciting exploration. The issue of financial giving has troubled Christians from the beginning of the church's existence. Jesus courageously addressed the topic in his time. Now you have chosen to address the question of giving—specifically, of tithing—in your life. Therefore, approach these next thirty days with anticipation, curiosity, openness, and humor.

You have agreed to make three commitments to one another during the coming month. I ask you to publicly affirm these now in front of this congregation.

Will you devote yourselves to reading and meditating on the assigned Scripture daily?
I will.

Will you meet with other members of the group every week to share the struggles and joys of the journey toward tithing?
I will.

Will you work with the group to form a covenant at the end of the thirty-day period to prayerfully make a decision about your next steps in establishing benchmarks for your giving?
I will.

Let us pray:
Almighty God, pour out your blessing upon these your servants who have

accepted the invitation to explore their faith in fresh ways over the next month. Guide them in their reading of your Word. Lead them in the decisions they make about their giving. Enable them to listen to one another and to encourage one another. Bless them in their journey of discipleship, through Jesus Christ, our Lord. Amen.

The members of the group return to their seats.

Offertory Ideas and $entences to Use During the Thirty-Day Period

The pastor plays a key role in encouraging and supporting the core group on their journey toward tithing. One way to support the group during the thirty-day journey, and to keep before the congregation the importance of financial stewardship, is to use the brief moments before the offering is gathered in the worship service to help the whole congregation focus on the relationship between God and humanity, symbolized by the tithe.

The pastor may say the following statements prior to the offering to reinforce the commitment of the core group over the next month, as well as to provide spiritual leadership to the whole congregation in its search for a deeper relationship with God. Of course, the pastor would want to adapt the statement to fit his or her congregation's needs and style.

Week 1

A terrible plague ravaged Israel. Over seventy thousand people died. King David took responsibility before God for the catastrophe. After David's confession and plea, a prophet named Gad instructed David to build an altar. A threshing floor, owned by a man named Araunah, was chosen for the site.

Araunah was thrilled that the king wanted to use his site for an altar, so he offered to give to David the site along with the oxen for the sacrifice. In 2 Samuel 24:24, we read: "But the king said to Araunah, 'No, but I will buy them from you for a price; I will not offer burnt offerings to the LORD my God that cost me nothing.'"

A significant offering costs us something. May you find the satisfaction in giving that which costs you today.

Week 2

Paul wrote a fundraising note to the church at Corinth. He started his communication with a report about the churches in Macedonia. Apparently the region was very poor—or, at least, the Christians in those churches were poor. Paul told the Corinthians that despite the Macedonian believers' poverty, their giving had "overflowed in a wealth of generosity" (2 Corinthians 8:2).

In our church, we have a group of people who are exploring ways in which they can grow toward generosity. A core group is engaged in daily prayer, Scripture reading, meditation, and weekly gatherings to explore the biblical call to joyful, generous giving.

All of us would like to be more giving than we are. Even though most of us are not part of this core group, each of us can prayerfully explore what it means to be generous and to set some benchmarks for our giving. May this act of worship through giving today be a significant step in spiritual growth for each of us as well as an act of encouragement to the core group.

Week 3

The Old Testament patriarch Jacob had a traumatic night. While running away from a family squabble, he slept in the outdoors, with a stone as his pillow. He dreamed of a ladder between heaven and earth, with angels going up and down on it. That same night Jacob wrestled with a heavenly being, and his hip was dislocated in the struggle. In the morning, Jacob erected an altar at the site and said, " . . . this stone, which I have set up for a pillar, shall be God's house; and of all that you give me I will surely give one tenth to you" (Genesis 28:22).

The tradition of giving one tenth of one's income is ancient. One tenth—a tithe—is a spiritually significant amount, not a mere token. It is a benchmark for giving, a goal to work toward and to move beyond.

As you give today, will you prayerfully take a step toward this historic benchmark for giving and seek God's guidance and the support of other Christians as you move along your spiritual journey?

Week 4

Do you remember the story about the diminutive tax collector named Zacchaeus, who climbed up in a sycamore tree? He wanted to get a good look at Jesus when Jesus came through his part of town. Jesus called Zacchaeus down from the tree and invited himself to Zacchaeus's home for dinner. There are many things about this story that we don't know but would like to know. One of the things I would like to know is, What did Jesus and Zacchaeus talk about at that meal?

But we only know the results. After the meal, Zacchaeus said, "Half of my possessions, Lord, I will give to the poor" (Luke 19:8a). A close relationship with Jesus changed a man's relationship to his financial resources. As you give today, prayerfully consider your relationship with Jesus and your relationship with your financial resources. Are both of these relationships what you want them to be? Take the first steps today toward realigning these relationships.

A Move Toward Whole-Life $tewardship:
Explaining the Ten-Week Process

Some core-group members who complete the initial thirty-day experiment will not want (or be able) to continue the next step of this spiritual journey. Many core-group members will want to proceed with the next step—the ten-week commitment for mutual support and growth. This ten-week pilgrimage of study, prayer, and reflection on giving will help participants persevere in their commitment and find mutual support in their journey toward whole-life stewardship.

Core-group members continuing for the next ten weeks will make the following commitments:

- to prepare an individual assessment of the percentage of income the person is now giving;
- to study and reflect upon the assigned Scripture passages for each of the ten weeks (see Appendix II);
- to gather weekly with members of the core group for discussion and prayer;
- to prepare an evaluation at the end of the ten-week period, including considering an invitation to continue to meet monthly for the next three months.

Getting Started

An orientation session should be held, led by the pastor (or someone the pastor designates). We strongly encourage the pastor to be the leader of the first group to embark on the ten-week experience. Following this first experience, another staff member or layperson who has participated in the first group, may be named as leader of the next group.

The purpose of the orientation session is to (1) determine the time and place of the weekly group meetings; (2) confirm who will lead the weekly sessions; (3) allow participants to develop their individual covenants; (4) make sure that participants understand the elements of the ten-week journey, particularly the weekly Scripture readings (Appendix II).

The Covenant

This book concentrates on spiritual markers; particularly, it focuses on the tithe as a helpful benchmark for financial stewardship. However, no growth in discipleship can take place by isolating one area of life from all other areas. Therefore, as participants in the ten-week experiment develop their own covenants, they are called to remember that God asks for one hundred percent of our lives, not just ten percent. Financial giving, worship, service, talent, and time are all interrelated in our lives and part of our service to God. In writing the covenant, each participant should set benchmarks to work toward in as many areas of life as possible without becoming overwhelmed.

Each participant prepares his or her own covenant. The covenant centers on areas of spiritual growth the person wishes to focus on during the next ten weeks. No one should be expected to go on the journey alone; therefore, the covenant should name areas where encouragement and support would be helpful as the participant journeys toward whole-life stewardship.

Each person is held accountable for his or her own covenantal commitments—but not through authority imposed "from above." The person invites fellow group members to hold him or her accountable in a loving way. Each member invites every other member to sign his or her covenant. For this reason, participants should not list an item in the covenant that they do not want to be held accountable for.

The covenant below is a guide for members to consider in writing their own covenants; they should feel free to adapt it to their own needs. There is no right number of items to make up the covenant. Each person should cut or add items as he or she experiences God's nudging and leading.

Sample Covenant

By the grace of God, for the next ten weeks I will . . .
- pray each day for each person in my covenant group;
- pray daily for my church and my pastor;
- attend worship at least once each week;
- read the letters of Paul, especially Philippians and 2 Corinthians;
- read one Christian classic, for example *Mere Christianity,* by C. S. Lewis;
- raise my giving through the church by two percentage points of my income as I move toward the benchmark of the tithe;
- make a gift through the church out of my accumulated assets;
- volunteer one hour per week in a local ministry to those less fortunate than myself;
- prepare an estate plan around sound principles of Christian stewardship;
- spend twenty minutes each night talking with one of my children, a friend, or my spouse.

Signatures of spiritual friends who will encourage me as I move toward my benchmarks:
1. _____
2. _____
3. _____
4. _____
5. _____
6. _____

Individual Financial Assessment

Although an individual financial assessment is rarely shared with others, preparing the assessment is an important spiritual discipline for each group member. It is a reality check for the participant.

To prepare the assessment, the member (with spouse or significant other) reviews his or her personal financial transactions for a one-month period, asking questions such as the following: What was my total monthly income? How much did I spend during the month and on what items or services? How much money did I save? How much did I give to the church?

Taking the actual figures from the review, the person divides the amount given to the church by the total monthly income. This provides the percentage of total income given to the church for the month. The member prayerfully assesses his or her giving by asking questions such as, How do I feel about the amount I have given? Am I moving toward my goal for giving? Am I able to thank God for being able to contribute the amount I have given during the month? If the person finds his or her reflections on these questions disturbing, he or she can take another look at the total expenditures and ask questions such as, What do these expenditures tell me about my priorities? Do I need help to make changes in priorities? Do I need professional financial counseling? Should I ask the rest of the group to hold me accountable and to support me with prayer? The important thing for the person is not to wallow in guilt but to make concrete plans about how to move toward new goals.

Study and Reflection

During each week of the ten-week period, participants will immerse themselves in the designated Scripture passage. They should read the passage each day of the week and use the reflection questions as a way to discern God's guidance about stewardship, particularly the spiritual discipline of tithing. The designated Scripture passages are found in Appendix II, pages 109–112.

Weekly Group Meetings

The weekly meetings of the group may be led by the pastor or by someone designated by the church leadership. Some groups choose to provide their own leadership on a rotating basis. Each group should determine an appropriate system of leadership prior to the first meeting of the group.

The group may meet at the church, in a home, or in a restaurant. The only requirement is that the location provide privacy. It is important to meet at the same time and place for the ten-week period.

Each meeting may be from sixty to ninety minutes in length. If the group has more than five members, the meeting should be ninety minutes long. It is important that the length for the sessions be agreed upon before the first session.

We recommend the following format for the sessions:

- Open the session with a brief centering prayer.
- Allow each person to report on one victory or one challenge that he or she has experienced during the week. Allow no more than five minutes for each participant to speak.
- Discuss the assigned Scripture passage for the week. Ask: "What insights did you receive?"
- Review the reflection questions about grace, giftedness, giving, and growth. Ask: "In reflecting on these questions, what insights did you receive that troubled or disturbed you?"
- Invite each person to share a prayer request. Encourage participants to focus their requests on issues related to the covenants.
- Close the session with prayer.

Evaluation and Invitation

At the end of the ten-week period, the leader should invite the group to spend at least one hour evaluating the experience. The group may use questions like these to do the assessment:

- What went well during this ten-week experience?
- What did we learn?
- What could be improved about the way the information about the ten-week experience was shared with the congregation? about the instructions for the sessions?
- How can we share what we have learned from this experience with others in the church and in other settings?
- Do we wish to continue with monthly meetings so that we may encourage one another and hold one another accountable?

Holy $moke in Your Church

A Theological Rationale for the Ten-Week Period

Tithing is not about raising money; it is about discipleship. Tithing does not focus on the church budget; it is a spiritual discipline that focuses on Jesus Christ. When tithing is separated from spiritual growth, it becomes spiritual snobbery.

The Living Bible's paraphrase of Deuteronomy (14:23c) states, "The purpose of tithing is to teach you always to put God first in your lives."[2] When

---

2 Taken from *The Living Bible*, copyright © 1971. Used by permission of Tyndale House Publishers, Wheaton, Illinois 60189. All rights reserved.

God is first in our lives, that changes everything. Of course, all through human history, a few people have chosen tithing for other purposes. The evidence of misuse is seen in the confrontations Jesus had with Pharisees. However, we don't throw out a good gift just because some folks use it in wrong ways. For most people, money is the last line of defense between the heart and God.

When God is first in our lives, everything is transformed. Since Bible times, the effects of the tithe have gone in three directions:

■ *Tithing affects the one who tithes.*

You can't provide from the well unless there is something in the well. You can't build a bonfire unless you have fuel to burn. If tithing is a spiritual discipline, it is a method of adding power to the inner life so that there is something to give.

■ *Tithing affects the community and the community of faith.*

An act of generous giving is a powerful witness in our culture. Tithing may mean the reordering of priorities in your life. It can help bring about change of all kinds in the society around us. Tithing is a profound witness for the reign of God.

■ *Tithing affects the needy.*

Concern for the indigent and powerless is a consistent theme through-out the whole Bible. The agricultural tithe of early Hebrew history was a method of seeing to it that everyone had enough to eat. Modern Americans tend to separate spirituality from direct action. Our spiritual ancestors would be totally confused by the separation. When they failed to keep the two together, judgment came upon them. The prophet Amos reprimanded the people for their sacrifices and tithes while the needy were pushed to the side. (See Amos 4:1, 4-5; 5:21-24.)

Many people begin tithing because of a sense of inner responsibility to share what they have with those who have less. The tithe becomes a helpful benchmark for them to fulfill an inner urge—which we believe is prompted by the Spirit of God.

General Helps

The following is a potpourri of options that the pastor and other lead-ers in the congregation can use to strengthen an awareness about stewardship, giving, and tithing and to support the group journeying toward whole-life stewardship. Not every option will fit every congrega-tion. Leaders should choose the options most appropriate to their congregation's life. Indeed, some of these options may spark even better ideas to use in the congregation.

Sermon Ideas

- If you use the Revised Common Lectionary, look at each appointed Scripture passage to see if there are economic and justice dimensions.
- Preach a series of sermons on assigned readings in this journey for each week.
- Review the sermons in Brian K. Bauknight's book *Right on the Money: Messages for Spiritual Growth Through Giving* (Discipleship Resources, 1998). Use insights from this reading in preparing your sermons.
- Read the book *Preaching For Giving: Proclaiming Financial Stewardship With Holy Boldness*, by Timothy J. Bagwell (Discipleship Resources, 1998), and use insights and ideas from the book in preparing your sermons.

Worship

- For each of the ten weeks, select a person to give a testimonial or to witness about his or her pilgrimage of giving.
- Develop a series of invitations to giving that will make the offering more celebratory during the ten-week period.
- Invite members of the group pursuing the ten-week journey to offer the prayer of dedication of the offering.

Christian Education

- Develop a series of Sunday school lessons on stewardship and giving for all ages. Contact the stewardship staff at the General Board of Discipleship of The United Methodist Church for recommended studies. Write to Congregational Leaders Team, The General Board of Discipleship, P.O. Box 340003, Nashville, TN 37203-0003; or e-mail hmather@gbod.org.
- Provide classes for parents to help them communicate to their children healthy Christian values about money.

Spiritual Life Committee

- Create opportunities for parishioners to think about the relationship between money and faith.
- Invite a twelve-step group of "Spenders Anonymous" to use the facilities of your church.

Family Life Group

- Plan a Sunday-afternoon or weekday-evening session on personal and family financial planning, using *Christians and Money: A Guide to Personal Finance*, by Donald W. Joiner (Discipleship Resources, 1991), or another suitable resource.
- Include families in planning alternative, low-expense fun nights for family groups from the church and community.

- Set up a series of classes using the video series *Master Your Money*. (Available from Walk Through the Bible Ministries, Inc., P.O. Box 80587, Atlanta, GA 30366; or call 404-458-9300.)
- Prepare a special session on planned giving. Ideas for such a session are available from the Planned Giving Resource Center, P.O. Box 340003, Nashville, TN 37203-0003.
- Involve people from the congregation in special ministries with the poor in your community.

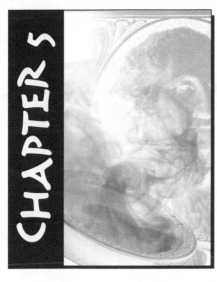

CHAPTER 5

Letting Your Whole Life Go Up in $moke!
Planned Giving and the Tither

The land of a rich man produced abundantly. And he thought to himself, "What should I do, for I have no place to store my crops?" Then he said, "I will do this: I will pull down my barns and build larger ones, and there I will store all my grain and my goods. And I will say to my soul, 'Soul, you have ample goods laid up for many years; relax, eat, drink, be merry.'" But God said to him, "You fool! This very night your life is being demanded of you. And the things you have prepared, whose will they be?"

(Luke 12:16-20)

Throughout this book we have urged pastors and other church leaders to remember the purpose of the tithe: The tithe is not a way to give one tenth of our lives and our resources to God, but a discipline to remind us and enable us to allow God to reign over one hundred percent of our lives and our substance. Giving does not need to end when we die. Church leadership has not done a good job in communicating that fact or the opportunities for giving to continue.

If we believe in the Resurrection—that there is life after life—part of our stewardship responsibility is to ensure that the possessions entrusted to us will continue to be invested in ways consistent with our values and hopes. Horror stories and court documents attest to battles over inheritances. Families have been torn apart. Inheritances have ended up in situations that were far different from the hopes and dreams of the deceased. Sometimes estates have been used irresponsibly. That does not need to happen, and we can do something about it.

No plan, or an inadequate plan, for the disposition of our earthly goods has the same consequences as hoarding. And, generally, hoarding is called sin. At the end of life, a person often has more possessions than ever before. The choice is to use them wisely or to use them foolishly. If we take seriously the word that "to whom much has been given, much will be required" (Luke 12:48), then we know that God has significant expectations for most of us at the end of our days. We have the opportunity to plan for the best, most sensible use of all that we have received. Our Lord wants our estates to be turned into holy smoke and not to be consumed by courts and governments.

$ad But True (Only the Names Have Been Changed)

The tithe is a helpful guide (benchmark) for planning our estates. However, estate planning is a much larger issue, as almost everything is. We provide two real-life stories to explain what we mean.

■ ■ ■

Bob and Martha Miller were a fine couple. They generously supported their church with their money and their talents. Throughout his seventy-four years, Bob lived an exemplary life in the community. He and Martha and their two sons were considered a model family.

Bob's wife died when Bob was seventy years of age. At that point Bob determined to devote his remaining days to strengthening his business so that his two sons could continue the family tradition and support their families with a business they knew and loved. Bob had a picture in his mind of handing the keys over to them as he walked out the door to retire to a life of fishing and golf.

His pastor was his friend and confidant. Bob told the pastor of his dream. But the dream never came to fruition. One evening while driving home, Bob felt a severe tightening in his chest. In pain, he released the steering wheel; the car smashed headlong into a huge tree. Bob lived only a few minutes. At the funeral the pastor said, "If anyone was ever prepared to go in an instant, it was Bob." Everyone thought this was surely correct.

A few months went by. One day the Internal Revenue Service sent Bob's sons a letter notifying them that the outstanding tax bill on their father's estate was nearly $800,000. How could this be? Bob lived comfortably, but no one considered him rich. His sons had received about $250,000 each from certificates, insurance, and other investments their father had made. How could there be a bill for $800,000?

The problem is, no one had bothered to check on the law regarding estate taxes. Everything of value that the deceased owned was included in the taxable property. The business inventory of machines and warehouses was worth over $1 million. Once Bob and Martha's home, furniture, silverware, paintings, shotguns, library, and jewelry were added in, the estate was valued at well over $2 million!

The tax bill stunned the sons. How could they possibly pay it! They could cover some of it with the cash assets their father had left them; but after funeral expenses, attorney's fees, and other debts, this only covered about half of the bill. Even if they sold the old homeplace and personal items, they would still be considerably short.

With great sadness, the sons sold the business their father had thought he was leaving to them. They could find no other option to satisfy the tax bill. Once sold, the proceeds paid the estate tax plus some capital gains tax. While no amount could soothe aching hearts, the small amount left for the sons felt like an insult. They not only lost their parents but also a dream. The pastor was quick to console them. He assured them that they just had no other choice. They had done everything they could. The words were correct for the sons; however, the father could have done many things prior to his death to avoid this tragic outcome. Good stewardship planning by the father before he died could have radically changed the whole scenario. Words on paper would have made all the difference in the world.

Bob Miller thought he was a good steward—and, in many ways he was. He and Martha taught their sons to care for life and to care for the world. Their church had led them to tithe and even to give offerings beyond the tithe. Bob was a generous man. When it came to the steward-ship of acquired assets, however, no one provided guidance for either Bob or his children.

A local stockbroker often held workshops, and a lawyer regularly advertised his seminars on estate planning; but Bob saw both of those as advertising to sell their own products and services. He was a person of faith and trusted that all would work out all right. Everything he had heard in sermons and read from his faith community assured him that he was doing the right thing in terms of Christian financial stewardship. He tithed. What more could be done? Sadly, the church let him down without even knowing it. The church only taught financial stewardship of *current* income. It was silent about *accumulated assets*.

The failure to teach people within the congregation about planned giv-ing is a serious lapse in the responsibility of church leadership. We live in a strange day when some people claim that the church has a responsibility to teach morally responsible behavior in marriage but think that responsible financial management is "too personal" to be talked about in public. Planned giving is an important ingredient for developing a whole lifestyle; it is a decision-making task of the Christian.

■ ■ ■

One pastor relayed this all-too-real story of how she learned of the necessity of knowing and teaching about planned giving.

The church secretary came into the office to ask a question: "Reverend Kate, we have received a check from a Mr. John Burns for five hundred dol-lars. Do you know him?"

The pastor did know him. "He is the nephew of Mrs. Lloyd, who died a short while ago. We got well acquainted during my visits to his aunt at the hospital. He is not a member here or anywhere else, if I remember correctly. I will call him and see if this is a memorial gift."

Reverend Kate called Mr. Burns and inquired about the check. She asked if Mr. Burns wanted to designate it for a memorial or for anything else in particular.

"Just put it anywhere you want, Preacher; I was just feeling sorry for you and the church, that's all." The pastor did not exactly know how to take that last statement. She was pleased to have discretion about where to use the funds but did not understand why Mr. Burns felt sorry for the church. She soon found out.

"Reverend, you know that Auntie had no children. She never married— unless you want to call the school her husband. Teaching was her whole life, for forty years. She lived simply and saved most of what she made. Giving to the church was a high priority for her, but not much else. Anyway, she did not have a will. While lying up in the hospital, she heard one of those television preachers talk about how someone could leave their money to that ministry in their will. Auntie had never thought much about what to do with her money after she was gone.

"She didn't have a will. She called a lawyer to come out to the hospital and write up her first and only will. She gave all her money to this television man she had never met. I asked her why she had not chosen to give the money to the church she loved so much. Her answer was that she never thought about it. The church had never asked for it.

"I urged her to change the will, and she asked me to get the lawyer back out there. She died that night. Yesterday the attorneys sent a check for over half a million dollars to those television people. I just felt sorry for you."

Reverend Kate understood why Mr. Burns felt sorry for the church. The pastor felt sorry for her church too. The amount of money would have enabled considerable ministry to be done in their small community. It did not help her feelings any when the man on television was arrested and sent to prison only four months later. Those funds probably were not used to enhance the love and justice seen in Jesus. An opportunity to turn an estate into holy smoke was lost.

Mrs. Lloyd loved the church and attended regularly. She had been a tither almost all of her life. At no point along her faith journey, however, did anyone ever discuss planned giving with her. This wonderful school teacher had only heard a part of the story. She was denied the opportunity to make a gift that could have been used to make a difference for generations. It was not her fault.

An Uncertain Future . . . The Fire Is Going Out

In Chapter 1 we explained a few alarming facts raised about church giving. These facts call attention to the need to vigorously urge planned giving in every congregation. There has never been a more opportune time in the history of giving. There is no benefit to blaming the potential givers; it is up to the church to cast a vision of ministry that grasps the imaginations of those with accumulated assets.

In the book *Behind the Stained Glass Windows*, John and Sylvia Ronsvalle note: "Giving patterns in the United States indicate the church is losing market share among its own members. Even many denominations that are growing in membership are receiving a smaller portion of their members' incomes."[1]

Noted author and chaplain of Duke University William Willimon was quoted in *The Mainline Church's Funding Crisis* as saying that congregations today are looking at a financial crisis unparalleled in scope.[2] Whether the financial crisis leads to spiritual health or terminal illness is unknown.

Research done by *Giving USA*, a major reference text on philanthropy in America, has revealed that the proportion of charitable funds given to religion continues to shrink each year. For several decades, religious giving was well above fifty percent of *all* benevolent giving in America. Today it is about forty-five percent of the total.[3]

Many large givers are donating huge sums to a variety of institutions and agencies. They give to a dream. The organizations communicate a vision. We are convinced that the reason much of the giving has not been coming to the church is that the vision we have cast is to meet the annual budget. Institutional survival does not make holy smoke.

In many congregations, people who contribute the largest amounts of money are those over seventy years of age. It is not uncommon for fifty percent or more of the total support of the church to come from the retirees. These are the people who were children during the Depression or were raised by people for whom the Depression was a vivid memory. They were taught frugality and giving; the two went together. Because of that combination, many experts believe that fifteen trillion dollars will be handed over to a new generation during the next twenty years. A large percentage of this will likely go to pay estate taxes.

Remember, those who manage the assets now are generous people. They

1 From *Behind the Stained Glass Windows: Money Dynamics in the Church*, by John Ronsvalle and Sylvia Ronsvalle (Baker Books, 1996); page 29.

2 *The Mainline Church's Funding Crisis: Issues and Possibilities*, by Ronald E. Vallet and Charles E. Zech (William B. Eerdmans Publishing Company, 1995); page xiii.

3 *Giving USA: The Annual Report on Philanthropy for the Year 1997*, edited by Ann E. Kaplan (AAFRC Trust for Philanthropy, 1998); page 23.

tend to be loyal to the church and seek to be faithful to the call of Christ as they understand the call through the Scriptures. These people are givers. So the church must help them do what they want to do: give.

Many pastors grew up poor and never accumulated any assets of note. And since most pastors live in church-owned housing, they may not even think much about capital gains and the power of inflation on assets. For these and other reasons, it is not unusual for pastors to be oblivious to the fact that many of their church members have accumulated quite a few assets during their lifetimes. These people may not have a very large cash flow, but they may be "worth a lot." These members need and deserve sound Christian education on proper stewardship of their estates.

Planned giving allows people to find joy in giving, both while they are alive and while they are arranging for their estate to be invested in those values that are dear to them. People rarely give to the church or to any other charitable organization merely to get a tax reduction. However, planned giving may make it possible for individuals to give much more to the church or to charity than would have been possible without the technical knowledge.

Planned giving focuses on alternative ways to give while living as well as through estate planning. Teaching the basics of planned giving and inviting people to consider new options for giving can be a win-win situation. The givers can find fulfillment in giving to support the values that they have been supporting all of their lives.

How many congregations do some planned giving?[4]	
Budgets over $200,000	59%
Budgets between $100,000 and $199,000	48%
Budgets under $100,000	39%
All churches	43%

In addition, because the church has been a primary value to these folks, we anticipate that much of the directed giving through estates will be channeled through the churches. The church has the potential for a more stable income for its mission and ministry than it has ever experienced previously.

Many prognosticators believe that the Baby Boomer generation will not be a giving generation. Current data on church giving shows that they are far behind their parents and grandparents in giving. Only the passage of time will tell for sure. We do not believe that it is foreordained that Baby Boomers will not be givers as they move into their retirement years—but they have a long way to go.

4 From *How to Increase Giving in Your Church*, copyright 1997 Regal Books, Ventura, CA 93003. Used with permission; page 179.

An older generation in the United States is dying and leaving a large hole unfilled in churches all across the nation. We are sure that the Boomers (born between 1946 and 1964) and the Busters (born between 1965 and 1981) will not be givers unless they are taught and invited. By teaching, we do not mean that they will respond to argument or to a stack of "facts." Boomers like to experience things.

When Carlos and Jacque drew up their will, they designated that a major portion of the estate is to go to a church foundation. Their children are to select the projects to receive the funds. The only stipulation in the will is that the funds must be used to assist the needy. The will provides the children of the deceased an opportunity to learn more about giving even after the parents' death.

Chapter 4 of this book is designed to provide people like them an opportunity to experience the joy of giving for themselves. The primary reason for developing the experiential covenant in Chapter 4 is to provide people who are unfamiliar with tithing an opportunity to test it out. They can work out the plan from within rather than seeing something imposed on them from outside.

While churches are teaching stewardship to a new generation, how does the church pay the bills *and* continue the ministry? One answer is by enabling the older generation to practice planned giving and leave a wonderful legacy behind to support the church during the transition.

Planned-Giving Basics

It is not important that the pastor or the lay leaders of a church become technical experts in planned giving. The process is complicated and is frequently changed by laws made in federal and state legislatures. Experts are available from many denominational agencies or in the local communities. Make use of them!

Those who have the technical skills and experience in planned giving are usually willing to be leaders for programs as well as for providing guidance on letters and promotional materials. Attempting to fulfill the role without proper knowledge can be disastrous—and often illegal.

However, we do not believe that the lack of any specific instructions about planned giving in the Bible should scare people off. The biblical writers could not have imagined the intricacies of state and federal law in the United States of America at the end of the millennium. Nor could they have imagined that most people would live into retirement years. In fact, the idea of retirement would not have made sense to the people of Bible times. The reasons for including planned giving in the life of the steward are the same as for any other kind of giving. In that sense, the reasons are biblical, even if the particulars are not.

Consider these basics of planned giving.

We Give It All Anyway!

The question is whether we will intentionally transfer the stewardship of what God has given us or allow the secular laws to make the final decisions. The fact is, we will not take any of our assets with us when we die. When our life ends on this earth, all our possessions will remain here, whether we like it or not. If we do not make a plan for distribution of the accumulation of our life's assets, someone else will make that all-important determination. Rather than the assets being turned into holy smoke, there is a good chance that those gifts will be consumed in ways that are not in line with our values.

The Simple Will

The most basic of planned giving instruments is the simple will. It is an inexpensive document to prepare. A will is a final statement by the deceased regarding what he or she wants done with all that was under his or her charge. This includes money, real estate, silverware, jewelry, minor children—even the dog. For younger families, the most important part of the will is often the description of what will happen to the children in case of the death of both parents. If one does not have a will (and sixty percent of Americans do not), the estate is divided by the court according to the law of the state. Not having a will means not assuming responsibility for what God has blessed you with, including your children. So make a will, and keep it up to date.

Estate Taxes

All estates with a value of more that $650,000 in 1999 (increasing at $25,000 a year) are taxed at a very high rate. The Tax Relief Act of 1997 gave some people the impression that the estate tax trap had been eliminated. For many people this was not the case. It is true that the amount of estate exempt from tax liability will increase over several years; however, there is no assurance that the increase will be aligned with the inflation rate.

Many family businesses and farms get immediate relief because they can leave up to $1.3 million before taxes are assessed. But this will provide little assistance to large holdings of real estate that may be producing limited cash flow. Remember, Uncle Sam counts dirt, animals, silverware, and almost anything else you can think of for its cash value. Estate taxes begin at around thirty-seven percent and quickly rise to over fifty-five percent.

A Living Trust or Credit-Shelter Trust

A living trust or credit-shelter trust is an instrument that helps individuals double the amount they can shelter from estate taxes. It involves removing a portion of one's estate and placing it in trust for one's children or others. People can do this and still utilize all the revenue generated by the trust.

This instrument is also quite valuable in allowing people to bypass the probate process and immediately turn assets over to loved ones. It also is a private document, whereas a will is a public document. A person can maintain privacy with a trust, if that is an important issue to the person.

Unlimited Marital Deduction

The government allows us to leave an unlimited amount to a spouse. None of this amount is subject to estate tax. This allowance causes many people to relax and assume that all is well. However, appropriate estate planning is important, because upon one's death the surviving spouse is significantly limited as to his or her planning options. When the second member of the household dies, children will get a significant tax hit and have little recourse.

Gifts to the Church

Any amount given to a church or charity before or at the time of death is completely removed from an estate. Often this allows a person to give a gift and have the government pay half or more than half of the gift for them through the savings in taxes. If the gift is given while the donor is still living, not only does the gift save on future estate taxes, but the donor also receives an immediate tax deduction for the gift on any taxes owed on ordinary income. This can double or triple what one otherwise might be able to give. It creates a lot more holy smoke!

Charitable-Remainder Trust

A charitable-remainder trust is one of the most exciting instruments known in planned giving. It is a great tool for people who have significant appreciated assets other than cash that may not be providing much cash flow but that would be highly valued in an estate. If these assets were sold, the appreciated value (the difference between what was paid for the asset and its current worth) would be subject to federal capital gains tax of at least twenty percent, plus state capital gains. By establishing a trust, people can give the asset to a church and avoid capital gains tax, and they receive a significant tax deduction. This deduction is placed into a life-insurance trust for the children to receive when the person dies.

The church can sell the asset and will not have to pay any tax, thus allowing it to invest one hundred percent of the value. The church then takes the income from the invested funds and returns it to the donor for as long as the donor lives, helping the cash flow. When the person dies, the church keeps the invested money for its missional purposes, and the heirs receive the insurance trust. Everyone wins!

Failure to use the charitable-remainder option can leave an estate tax burden and only about half of the expected inheritance for heirs. Taking advantage of the option means the church receives a major gift, thus allowing the church to make lots of holy smoke.

This brief review of options does not pretend to make estate-planning experts or planned-giving professionals out of the readers. We wanted to bring enough information that you will see the value and even the necessity of communicating planned giving to congregations. Literally billions of dollars that God could transform into holy purposes are lost every year. Any good training program designed to create more faithful stewards in the church will see that planned giving is a vital component.

Holy Smoke! What Do I Do Next?

A planned-giving program is not difficult to bring into the congregation's ministry. It involves education, more education, and continuous education. Simply put, pastors do not have to be experts at all; but they do have to provide members with the tools for planned giving. The members will figure out for themselves which tools apply to them.

Successful churches that receive a number of planned gifts offer frequent teaching seminars and mailings regarding the variety of possibilities members should consider as good stewards of their resources. Quarterly meetings and mailings are the general methods and should be sufficient.

A small task group of laypeople in the congregation can coordinate the planned-giving effort. They don't have to understand the intricacies of it all. They can contact a denominational official or a planned-giving professional in the community for expertise in planning a twelve-month comprehensive program for the congregation. Professionals can direct the task group to brochures and pamphlets that can be mailed to homes between seminars.

Planned-giving programs usually take several years before they begin to produce financial results. Once the money comes in from the efforts, it becomes contagious for a congregation. Simply announcing the reception of a gift helps promote the process and encourages other people to join in.

Before launching a planned-giving program, the task force should prepare an important document called an Endowment Policy. This policy should cover such important areas as (1) who will manage the gifts, (2) how gifts will be designated, (3) how the principle will be protected, and (4) what the interest earned will be used for. Again, guidelines for this uncomplicated but important document can be obtained from denominational offices.

The task force should thoroughly investigate the real possibility that people in the congregation have no holy smoke plan for their resources after their death. It is very sad when, upon the death of a generous Christian, his or her assets are channeled into actions and activities that are not aligned to his or her values. Trillions of dollars that could go toward feeding the hungry, sheltering the homeless, empowering the poor, and caring for the helpless are diverted away from those who were the focus of Jesus' ministry. Such assets could have been turned into holy smoke.

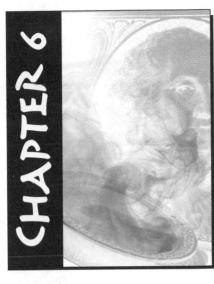

CHAPTER 6

The Big Bonfire:
The Holy $moke of a Capital Campaign

"A capital campaign is a concentrated effort by an organization or institution to raise a specified sum of money to meet a specified goal within a specified period of time."

Thomas E. Broce[1]

In preparing this book we were surprised at the number of questions people asked us about capital campaigns. For example, "Wouldn't we have all the money we need if everyone tithed?" Or, "If you develop a tithing church, should you still have capital campaigns?" Or even, "Should we even ask tithers to participate in a capital campaign?"

Questions like these helped us to further understand how people misunderstand tithing, the tither, and the mission of the church. We also saw how many people have no idea why capital campaigns are held or how they are run. Let's take the issue of the mission of the church. When a person asks, "Wouldn't we have all the money we need if everyone tithed?" he or she is suggesting that the mission of the church is to meet the budget. But the purpose of the church is to make disciples of Jesus Christ for the transformation of the world. We don't urge people to tithe in order for the church to meet its bills. Tithing is a spiritual discipline that helps the tither grow in grace *while at the same time* making available funds to feed the hungry, heal the sick, and provide shelter for the homeless. The church is always the instrument, never the end. A good capital campaign is just one more tool to assist the church in making disciples.

Second, tithing and capital campaigns go together well. They should go together for the good of the individual and the good of the church's ministry. Most local-church leaders discover that those who tithe are the ones who lead in a capital campaign. Why? Because tithing is not primarily about money; it's about priorities and spiritual power. If a capital campaign is about

1 From *Fund Raising: The Guide to Raising Money from Private Sources*, Second Edition, by Thomas E. Broce (University of Oklahoma Press, 1987); page 44.

service to the Kingdom, those most committed to the Kingdom will be the leaders. Unfortunately, most decision makers in the church do not give these tithers the opportunity to do what they need to do. Capital campaigns can fulfill that role.

In this book, we have encouraged you to view tithing as a benchmark to work toward and then *go beyond*. The capital campaign can be the steward- ship tool that enables people to do just that. The spiritual discipline of giving is not complete unless it includes all three pockets of wealth: the earned-income pocket for annual gifts; the accumulated-income pocket for capital gifts; and the estate pocket for planned gifts. In this section we will emphasize pocket number two: capital gifts.

The Lord Owns Our Acquired Assets Too, Preacher!

One pastor we know shared this all-too-true story with us. If occurrences like this did not happen so often, the story might actually be humorous.

The church this pastor was serving found itself in the midst of a five- month capital campaign to secure funds for classrooms and a new family-life center. The pastor was beginning to feel considerable stress about whether the effort would succeed—particularly in light of the most recent report of the committee on finance. With a snarl on his face, the treasurer noted that all bills were paid, leaving $6.20 in the church's bank account. He remarked later that this amount could be applied to the new building project (which he objected to). Our pastor friend was not having a good day. The congre- gation needed more than $800,000 for the building project, and it had a bit over $6 to apply toward it.

About the time the pastor thought all was lost, a long-time parishioner walked into his office. The man was a retired operator of a lumberyard. He had been successful in business and now spent a great deal of time helping out with the plant operations at the church. He and his wife had been near the top in annual giving for many years. The pastor was fairly certain that they were tithers.

After a brief bit of small talk, the retired church member said that he and his wife had a check to help kick off the building project. He wanted to know if the pastor wanted it or if he should just give it to the financial secretary.

The pastor did not mind receiving it and promised to get it to the finan- cial secretary. He appreciated the gesture by the retired businessman but was sure that it couldn't amount to anything monumental. After all, this fam- ily had already given in an exemplary fashion. How much more could they do? The pastor looked down at the check as it was handed to him. It was for $100,000. He nearly fainted!

As the pastor stood speechless, the retired lumberman said in a calm voice, "We have been waiting for the church to do something significant like this. Over the years we've accumulated many resources from the sale of our homes, our business, and some good investments. At this time in our lives, we're looking for ways the Lord wants us to properly use our assets. The church has always encouraged us to give ten percent of our income, and we have always done that. Until now, we have been given no real opportunity to use our acquired assets. The Lord owns them too, Preacher. Anyway, we're glad the church came up with this great project so that we could participate in it."

Understanding the $econd Pocket

Capital campaigns appeal to a different pocket than annual campaigns, but it is a pocket we *must* use for the mission and ministry of the church. When churches ignore accumulated assets, people are robbed of an opportunity and a blessing. Most of our churches teach only about the need to give a proportional share of earned income (salaries and retirement income); they ignore the other two pockets for giving. These are accumulated income—such as investments, property, and inheritances—and the "left-behind" pocket of estates. A person fully committed to God's mission in the world will want to give out of every pocket. The responsibility is upon the church to teach people how to give out of the other two pockets as well as to invite them to accept the opportunity.

The early Hebrews mentioned only crops and herds in their base for a tithe. Later, when the people settled and started raising olives and grapes, products such as oil and wine were included in the base. A generation or two ago, people could not conceive of anything but cash as the base for a tithe. But with the tremendous growth of the stock market in recent years, people can now consider tithing other assets as well.

In wrestling with the question about the relationship of tithers to a capital campaign, we issue the reminder again that tithing is not primarily about money but about the believer's relationship with God and with God's creation. Tithing is a life attitude. It is not a legalistic percentage to be met and camped upon but only a benchmark to help us measure our relationship with God and with the things of this world.

A capital campaign in a church does not center around money but around God's call for the congregation. The funds in a capital campaign may be essential for a congregation to fulfill its mission and ministry, but the funds are always simply a tool to accomplish the congregation's God-given mission. Financial success is one measure of a capital campaign, but it should never be the primary measure. Responding to the call of God is the ultimate yardstick.

In the Book of Numbers (chapters 13 and 14), there is a wonderful story about the report of the spies that Moses sent into Canaan. They came back with all the reasons why the Hebrews would not be successful if they tried to enter the Promised Land. The people that lived in Canaan were very strong, and their cities were well-fortified. In other words, the conquest looked impossible. Then Caleb said to the people, "Let us go up at once and occupy it, for we are well able to overcome it. . . . If the LORD is pleased with us, he will bring us into this land and give it to us" (Numbers 13:30; 14:8). In other words, if this is what God wants us to do, why are we even talking about anything else?

The Hebrew people decided to follow the report of the majority of the spies, deciding that they couldn't succeed. They did not consider whether *God* wanted them to enter the Promised Land.

Many congregations do the same sort of thing when it comes to deciding whether or not to have a capital campaign. The only questions they ask are, Can we afford it? What will it cost? How much interest will we have to pay? How much money do we have in the bank right now? They are more interested in protecting the pocketbook than in following the call into a new and exciting adventure in ministry. In other words, often churches corporately act like individuals who ask, "Can I afford to tithe?" However, the first question a congregation has to answer is, Who is calling us? If the response is that God is leading the church into a new ministry, then the next appropriate question is, What is the best tool for raising the funds that will make it possible to follow the Master?

Planning and Launching the Capital Campaign

When is it appropriate to use a capital campaign? This is never an easy question to answer, but some rules of thumb can be helpful. If (1) you have a firm project centered around a vision for ministry, and (2) you have not had a capital campaign for five years, then it may be an opportune time for one. The time during the year to have the campaign is also important. The two "windows of opportunity" for a capital campaign are spring and fall. Avoid holding capital campaigns in the middle of summer or during Advent or Holy Week.

In considering a capital campaign, it is important to assess the church's current debt. It is generally not wise to take on more than twenty-five percent of the annual operating budget in debt payments. A larger ratio of debt load runs the danger of limiting the other ministries of the church.

Most people who tithe are strongly committed to the mission and ministry of the church. If the church is so far in debt that it does not have the staff or program resources to minister in the community, the tither is discouraged. He or she is more likely to channel the tithe to some place where the mission is being carried out. Tithers are also people who have developed wise habits of spending and saving. When a congregation makes foolish borrowing decisions, the tither is turned off.

Some good practical questions to ask are: Will the capital campaign eliminate or reduce existing debt, or will it add to a current debt? If we do not use a capital campaign to accomplish what God wants us to do, what are our other options? (Remember: Not following God's call is not an option!) How often can we use a capital campaign? Initially, if you have not had a campaign in the last five years, you can have a very successful one. Two three-year campaigns can usually be held back to back without any problem. Three in a row is difficult unless the church has undergone significant membership growth.

Another significant factor in the decision about consecutive campaigns is the development of tithing within the congregation. We have stated that the largest amount of giving in a capital campaign will come from the accumulated assets of the tithers. Those who have given out of accumulated assets in previous capital campaigns are the ones most likely to give out of accumulated assets this time. Giving begets giving. However, if there are no new tithers since the last campaign, those who gave significantly in the last campaign may not have experienced enough appreciation of their assets to make as large a contribution as before. While one shouldn't assume that these contributors will not give again, one shouldn't be surprised if some of them don't make as significant a contribution as before.

An important question has to do with whether, in planning and conducting a capital campaign, a congregation should secure outside help. Occasionally a church has a gifted fundraising pastor or lay member, but this is rare. Our rule of thumb for most churches is that it is advisable to secure an outside consultant anytime the amount to be raised exceeds the annual budget. For large churches, the ratio is a bit different. For a church whose budget is between $500,000 and $1 million, we believe outside counsel should be acquired to help the church secure an amount of ninety percent or more of the budget. For a church whose budget is in excess of $1 million, a consultant will help it secure any amount exceeding eighty percent of the operating budget.

Consultants not only help the church be much more successful in raising dollars, but they also help maintain unity in the congregation during a potentially stressful time.

THE FIRST CAPITAL CAMPAIGN: WHAT RESULTS!

And they came, everyone whose heart was stirred, and everyone whose spirit was willing, and brought the Lord's offering to be used for the tent of meeting, and for all its service, and for the sacred vestments. So they came, both men and women; all who were of a willing heart brought brooches and earrings and signet rings and pendants, all sorts of gold objects . . . And everyone who possessed blue or purple or crimson yarn or fine linen or goats' hair or tanned rams' skins or fine leather, brought them. . . . All the Israelite men and women whose hearts made them willing to bring anything for the work that the Lord had commanded by Moses to be done, brought it as a freewill offering to the Lord. . . . The artisans who were doing every sort of task on the sanctuary came, each from the task being performed, and said to Moses, "The people are bringing much more than enough for doing the work that the Lord has commanded us to do." . . . So the people were restrained from bringing; for what they had already brought was more than enough to do all the work.

(Exodus 35:21-23, 29; 36:4-7)

Do not underestimate the stress a capital campaign can bring. When the Israelites fled Egypt, they were excited. It wasn't long, though, before the journey across the desert began to get to them. Once times got rough, the people began to mutiny.

Similarly, a capital campaign is a long journey with a great deal at stake. It requires a lot of work and disruption of schedule for the pastor. It means major responsibility and many additional meetings for the key laypeople. If these people have not been down the road before, it is frightening to try to lead the pack.

An outside consultant often stands within "the multitude" (the congregation) and speaks the truth where the "hometown prophet" (the pastor) could not. A good consultant will keep the leaders focused on the mission of the church. And a well-chosen consultant will help the church secure far more funds for ministry than most people dreamed possible. In addition, a consultant can do a lot to help maintain unity and focus. Both of those issues are important to tithers.

A good consultant will focus more on ministry than on money. He or she should be a stewardship professional and not just a fundraising professional. Tithers will recognize the difference.

How much money should a church expect to receive from a well-run capital campaign? That depends. Many factors are involved. The amount may run anywhere from one-and-a-half to five times the annual operating budget in three-year pledges. Factors that play a part are the age of the church, the age of the congregation, the type of project, the energy of the pastor, the spiritual maturity of the congregation, historic giving patterns, recognition of the vision, and the affluence of the membership.

People don't normally begin to tithe simply because they hear one sermon on tithing. In the same way, people rarely give generously out of their accumulated assets just because they're urged to do so on one occasion. That kind of miracle may happen, but it is rare. When someone has gone a lifetime without participating in holy smoke, it takes time and spiritual assistance through prayer, study, and discernment to make this big step. The foundations for giving out of current income and out of accumulated resources are the same. It is wise to invite those who have discovered meaning and joy in tithing their accumulated assets to share the story of their discovery with others.

The process leading up to a successful capital campaign is similar to the process for developing a congregation in which tithing becomes the benchmark for giving. Although there are differences in pace, the basics are related to one another. A capital campaign has five phases. Each is absolutely essential for success. In the brief description below, you will discover the steps that will help people who are moving toward the tithe, and those who already tithe, to begin to experience the Lordship of Christ over their accumulated assets as well as over their current income. Many will find a joy in giving that they never experienced before.

Vision. Before any campaign is conducted, there must be a vision of what God is calling the congregation to be and to do. It is essential that the vision be articulated by the pastor, accepted by lay leadership, and understood by the whole congregation. Unless people see how the capital campaign relates to the vision, there will be little enthusiasm. Find appropriate language to describe how this action will assist in making disciples of Jesus Christ.

Planning. A good capital campaign is in the planning phase for a year before people are asked to make a financial commitment. Six months before the commitments are sought, activities move into a higher gear. Dates are set and committees are carefully selected so that the congregation can be fully ready for the effort.

Leadership gifts. A capital campaign requires more than one kind of leadership. It is essential to have people who are willing to publicly take the lead in making a financial commitment. It is important to have concrete signs of support from a small minority of the church. Their willingness to venture out gives courage and raises the confidence level for others. Without individuals who are willing to lead, no one will know who to follow. Does anyone believe that the Hebrews would have moved across the desert if Moses, Aaron, and Joshua had not been willing to go first?

Public phase. After the initial, publicly committed gifts (from about fifteen percent of the congregation) have been received, it is imperative that a means be made possible for the rest of the congregation to follow.

Celebration. Rejoice and be glad! A capital campaign is a difficult journey, and ending it should be a time of celebration. Some people have made great sacrifices in both time and money. The celebration phase is often overlooked by churches who want to just sigh and move on. Let people shout and sing. Give them a chance to thank God in the company of the whole congregation and to reflect upon what God has enabled them to do.

A Concluding Word of Warning

We warned against manipulation when proclaiming, teaching, and urging people to establish the benchmark of tithing their income. In the same way, capital campaigns must be especially on guard against manipulation techniques. Guilt and coercion are never reasons to offer holy smoke. Holy smoke is a disciplined means of reminding us of the love of the Creator and our allegiance to God's purposes. Tithing and capital giving are both gracious acts. Any means to encourage gifts other than from the standpoint of what God is calling us to is inappropriate and unbiblical.

The capital campaign provides a wonderful opportunity for spiritual growth through giving. If the congregation's mission calls for a major step requiring finances, we rob ourselves and the whole people of God if we do not provide this opportunity for growth. Many congregations borrow funds and pay these back with interest. The interest payments could be better used for proclaiming the good news and feeding the hungry. Give people an opportunity to make holy smoke with their accumulated assets. It may well be the biggest spiritual bonfire your church has ever lit in the hearts of the people. We predict that tithers will be the first in line with the matches.

For Further Reading

Biblical and Theological Resources

Congregations at the Crossroads: Remembering to Be Households of God, by Ronald E. Vallet (William B. Eerdmans Publishing Company, 1998).

God The Economist, by M. Douglas Meeks (Augsburg/Fortress Press, 1989).

Let the Rivers Run: Stewardship and the Biblical Story, by Eugene F. Roop (William B. Eerdmans Publishing Company, 1991). This title is out of print. Check your church library or local library.

The Steward: A Biblical Symbol Come of Age, by Douglas John Hall (William B. Eerdmans Publishing Company, 1990). This title is out of print. Check your church library or local library.

Resources on Giving Research

Behind the Stained Glass Windows: Money Dynamics in the Church, by John Ronsvalle and Sylvia Ronsvalle (Baker Books, 1996).

Plain Talk About Churches and Money, by Dean Hoge, Patrick McNamara, and Charles Zech (The Alban Institute, 1997).

Resources on the Stewardship of Finances

Don't Shoot the Horse ('Til You Know How to Drive the Tractor): Moving From Annual Fund Raising to a Life of Giving, by Herb Mather (Discipleship Resources, 1994).

Money Isn't Is Everything: What Jesus Said About the Spiritual Power of Money, by Herb Miller (Discipleship Resources, 1994).

Revolutionizing Christian Stewardship for the 21st Century: Lessons from Copernicus, by Dan R. Dick (Discipleship Resources, 1997).

The Abingdon Guide to Funding Ministry: An Innovative Sourcebook for Church Leaders, edited by Donald W. Joiner (Abingdon Press, 1997).

Appendix 1

Scripture Readings for Each Day
of the Thirty-Day Experiment

Four themes are woven through the daily meditations that follow: grace, giftedness, giving, and growth. Spend a minimum of twelve minutes each day with the assigned Scripture passage, the selected reading from HOLY SMOKE!, and the questions provided. The questions and statements are meant to guide thinking about the biblical passages, not to limit how these Scriptures speak to you.

As you meditate, write down thoughts, insights, and questions. Record these in the spaces marked "Insights" and "Questions." Bring this book with you to each group session.

Day One
Genesis 1:1–2:4

Read this familiar passage as if you were in a spacecraft circling the earth. You look down at the blue planet. What new insights does this perspective provide?

Grace	What did it mean to God to make the creation? What has that to do with you?
Giftedness	What abilities do you have to take care of the creation?
Giving	How is the creation a gift of God? What gifts can you give?
Growth	What will you do today because of God's message through this passage?

Insights   Questions

Day Two
Job 38:4-41

God states some comparisons for Job in response to Job's complaints. Remember things you have complained about in the course of your life. How do they look now, years later?

Grace	Focus on what you have received rather than what you lack this day.
Giftedness	What responsibility comes from being part of God's creation?
Giving	How is creation a gift of God? What gifts can you give?
Growth	What difference will you make this day because of the message of God through this passage?

Insights   Questions

Day Three

Jeremiah 18:1-11

Recall a time when you watched a potter making an object at a wheel. No two articles of the potter's work are identical. Each is shaped in a unique way.

Grace	Consider experiences and events that have shaped your life.
Giftedness	What power and influence do you have to shape the materials of life around you?
Giving	In what ways will you invest your creativity?
Growth	What difference do you want this passage to make in your life?

Insights   Questions

Day Four

1 Chronicles 29:10-19

David offers a prayer at the dedication of the plans for the Temple. Think about prayer you have offered at the completion of an important task or project.

Grace	Is it hard to "feel" that everything comes from God? When does the sense that all is from God seem most real for you?
Giftedness	Can you feel good about some of your accomplishments? Name them.
Giving	If everything comes from God, what does that mean about your giving?
Growth	Name one thing you will do differently today because of your understanding that everything comes from God.

HOLY SMOKE! Read in Chapter 1 "A Tale of Holy Smoke," and "Measuring the Smoke," pages 7–12.

Insights   Questions

Day Five
Romans 8:18-28

"The whole creation has been groaning . . ." Consider how a problem
in one part of life creates problems in other parts. Also consider how
much joy and hope can come into life from unexpected sources.

Grace	How are you blessed by what is around you?
Giftedness	What good can you do for the whole creation?
Giving	In what ways can you heal the pain and travail in the world around you?
Growth	Name a "groaning" that you will act upon today, then act on it.

HOLY SMOKE! Read in Chapter 1 "The New Age May Drive Us to an Old Custom," pages 12–14.

Insights   Questions

Day $ix
Proverbs 3:5-10

The Book of Proverbs contains lots of pithy words of wisdom. Imagine
yourself sitting at the feet of a wise elder who gives you this advice.

Grace	One gift of God is that God is trustworthy. How do you depend upon God's trustworthiness?
Giftedness	How do you honor God?
Giving	Is giving a way to honor God? Giving what? Giving when? Giving how?
Growth	What will you do today because of the wisdom of this passage?

HOLY SMOKE! Read in Chapter 1 "Tithing in the Whole Scheme of Things" and "Instead of Burning Fat, We Are Getting Fat," pages 15–19.

Insights   Questions

Day Seven
1 Peter 4:8-11

Peter gives practical advice. Read these words as marching orders for the day.

Grace	When have you experienced love and hospitality as gifts?
Giftedness	Plan a specific way to extend love and hospitality today.
Giving	Plan one act of giving (time, money, influence, and so forth).
Growth	What difference do you want this passage to make in your life?

Insights   Questions

Holy Smoke!
Group Discussion of Chapter 1

Questions for discussion:

■ Are you concerned about church giving today?

■ Have you seen generational differences when it comes to attitudes toward giving?

■ How many people do you think practice tithing in your congregation?

■ What is your feeling when you hear the statement, "He's (or she's) a tither?"

Day Eight
Isaiah 40:27-31

*Have you ever been discouraged about the level of your maturity
as a Christian? Read these words of hope from the prophet Isaiah.*

Grace	Name ways in which God's power has come to you.
Giftedness	What would you do with the power and strength promised in the passage?
Giving	God gives power (verse 29). How can you empower (give power to) others?
Growth	Find a way to give someone hope today.

HOLY SMOKE! Read in Chapter 2 "The Tithe Before Abraham," pages 21–22.

Insights   Questions

Day Nine
Psalm 62

*Trust is the theme throughout this psalm. Who has been
trustworthy in your life? When have you been trustworthy?*

Grace	Trust is a gift. When have you been trusted?
Giftedness	In what ways can you express your trust in others?
Giving	Trust is a gift. Consider ways to provide that gift to someone else.
Growth	What difference do you want this psalm to make in your life today?

HOLY SMOKE! Read in Chapter 2 "The Tithe and the Old Testament," pages 22–27.

Insights   Questions

Day Ten
Romans 12:1-2

Culture urges us to conform. Nations and organizations (including churches) urge conformity. Paul urges transformation instead of conformity. Evaluate the contradictory pulls in your life.

Grace	One gift of grace is to be set free from conforming pressures. How would you know when you are free? Name the evidence of freedom you can think of.
Giftedness	What are the strengths and weaknesses within you that you yearn to see transformed by the power of God?
Giving	What would it mean to present your body as "a living sacrifice" (verse 1)? Have you ever given sacrificially?
Growth	What differences do you hope to experience in the transformed life?

Insights   Questions

Day Eleven
Luke 14:25-33

Do you tend to act on the spur of the moment, or do you act cautiously? How does having faith fit together with estimating the cost (see verse 28)? What major decisions do you anticipate in the next few months?

Grace	The ability to make decisions is a gift from God. Thank God for the gift.
Giftedness	What abilities do you have that enable you to make decisions?
Giving	Do you plan your giving, or is it a spontaneous, emotional reaction?
Growth	What difference would it make in your life if you estimated the cost more often?

HOLY SMOKE! Read in Chapter 2 "The Tithe and the New Testament," pages 27–29.

Insights   Questions

Day Twelve
Mark 4:35-41

Storms come into everyone's life. These storms are not all our own doing;
some simply happen. Consider the storms you have experienced.

Grace	Remember the peace that comes when the storm passes. Give thanks.
Giftedness	What would it mean to "wake up Jesus" in the midst of the storm?
Giving	Can awe be a gift? How would you express awe? Be specific.
Growth	What difference would it make in your life if Jesus calmed your fears (even about money)?

Insights   Questions

Day Thirteen
Luke 15:8-10

Recall a time when you found something that you had lost. How did you
feel? Did you tell others? What response did you receive from them?

Grace	What is of value to you? Do you think it will still be of value in ten years?
Giftedness	How is value added to your life and to the lives of others around you?
Giving	What do you have to share with others?
Growth	List values that restore relationships with people and with things that are eternally important.

HOLY SMOKE! Read in Chapter 2 "The Early Church and the Tithe" and "Recent History," pages 29–37.

Insights   Questions

Day Fourteen
John 15:1-15

In what ways are you connected with God? with others? with things? What do you love?

Grace	Name some good relationships that you did not initiate. Give thanks.
Giftedness	Name the gifts that you bring to a relationship.
Giving	How can you express love through giving?
Growth	Make a choice today that will deepen relationships with whatever is most important in your life.

Insights   Questions

Holy $moke!
Group Discussion of Chapter 2

Questions for discussion:
- What surprised you about the history of tithing?
- What do you make of the fact that Jesus rarely mentioned the tithe?
- What history does your family have with tithing?

Day Fifteen
Luke 16:19-31

Picture the scene in your mind. What separates people from one another today? Are economic differences the result or the cause of much of the separation?

Grace	Do you identify more with Lazarus or with the rich man? What benefits did each man enjoy?
Giftedness	What "crumbs" are under your table?
Giving	What do you have to give? Crumbs? Access? Relationships? Something else?
Growth	What does this passage call you to do differently?

HOLY SMOKE! Read in Chapter 3 "Is the Tithe Legalism?" pages 39–42.

Insights   Questions

Day $ixteen
Luke 12:22-34

What is of value to you? Look at your expenditures. What do your credit card statements say about what is important to you? What does the size of the check you write to your church say about what is important? How much is enough?

Grace	Name whatever is valuable to you that money cannot buy.
Giftedness	Identify something of value to you that you can share with others.
Giving	Does your giving reflect what you affirm as valuable?
Growth	Take a step toward reordering your life so that it aligns with the values you cherish.

HOLY SMOKE! Read in Chapter 3 "If Their Hearts Are Right, Won't the Money Come?" page 42.

Insights   Questions

Day Seventeen
Matthew 19:16-24
Have you ever lost something in a fire, a flood, or a
tornado? What possessions are important to you?

Grace	Where or how have you received the things that are most valuable to you?
Giftedness	What is there about you that cannot be given away but can be used for good in this world?
Giving	What could you give that would free you from a possession that possesses you?
Growth	What change is God calling you to make in your life?

HOLY SMOKE! Read in Chapter 3 "Is Social Security a Part of My Tithe?" pages 43–44.

Insights   Questions

Day Eighteen
Matthew 16:24-26
Is it hard to follow Jesus? What holds you back?

Grace	Relationships are the greatest of all gifts. Explore ways in which you experience God's love for you as a gift.
Giftedness	Identify what you bring to the relationship with God.
Giving	Give away something today that gets in the way of your relationship with God or with some of God's people.
Growth	What steps can you make today in order to "find" your life (verse 25)?

HOLY SMOKE! Read in Chapter 3 "Should the Whole Tithe Go to the Church?" pages 44–46.

Insights   Questions

Day Nineteen
Philippians 2:14-18

*Invest some time in thinking about murmuring, arguing, sacrificing,
and rejoicing. How is your faith an offering to God?*

Grace	Who are the people who have poured out (given) to you (verse 17)?
Giftedness	How can you rejoice with others?
Giving	Can you take a step toward tithing without murmuring or arguing?
Growth	Do an act of giving for which you can "be glad and rejoice" (verse 18).

HOLY SMOKE! Read in Chapter 3 "How Do I Figure the Tenth?" pages 46–48.

Insights   Questions

Day Twenty
Mark 12:41-44

*What is the biggest offering you ever made? As you read the story, don't focus
on the biggest dollar amount but on the most sacrificial gift you made.*

Grace	What is the most valuable thing you ever received? How did you "value" it?
Giftedness	Do you ever think, I have nothing to offer? You are a gift from God worth sharing! Share yourself today.
Giving	Make a sacrificial gift this week. Remember that sacrifice means "to make holy."
Growth	Map out a plan for growing as a giving Christian.

HOLY SMOKE! Read in Chapter 3 "Does the Tithe Include Time as well as Finances?" and "If Tithing Is a Benchmark, How Do I Know When I Have Reached the Pinnacle?" pages 48–51.

Insights   Questions

Day Twenty-One
2 Corinthians 8:6-8

Contrast the times when you felt compelled to give with times when you gave because you wanted to. What factors made the difference?

Grace	Count your blessings. Name them one by one.
Giftedness	You can only give what you have first received. Name what you have received.
Giving	What would it mean for you to give bountifully? Practice bountiful giving today.
Growth	Take one step toward being a cheerful giver.

Insights   Questions

Holy $moke!
Group Discussion of Chapter 3

Questions for the group:
- Is tithing legalism or a response of grace?
- What excuses do we make for not tithing?
- How do you plan to figure your tithe?
- Is tithing still valid?
- Do you have other benchmarks for giving in your life?

Day Twenty-Two
Romans 14:1-12

It is tempting to compare our giving with the giving of others. This passage suggests that we need to compare what we give with what we keep for our own use.

Grace	What have you received for which you can thank God?
Giftedness	How are you using the gifts you have received?
Giving	Take steps toward making your giving an affirmation of what you believe is really important.
Growth	Imagine standing before God and giving an account. Make a step today so that you will be able to make a better case before God.

HOLY SMOKE! Read in Chapter 5 the introduction and "Sad But True (Only the Names Have Been Changed)," pages 69–72.

Insights

Questions

Day Twenty-Three
2 Corinthians 8:1-7

Where have you seen generosity? In some Native American traditions, the one who is honored is not the one who accumulates the most but the one who gives away the most. How would you like to be honored and remembered?

Grace	Name ways in which you have been inspired.
Giftedness	If you gave yourself "first to the Lord" (verse 5), what would that require?
Giving	What does generous giving mean for you?
Growth	Take a step today to excel in a "wealth of generosity" (verse 2).

HOLY SMOKE! Read in Chapter 5 "An Uncertain Future . . . The Fire Is Going Out," pages 73–75.

Insights

Questions

Day Twenty-Four
1 Timothy 6:12-19
Consider the battles that go on within you. Do you ever
feel pride concerning your riches (or your simple living)?

Grace	What real treasure do you have? Name it.
Giftedness	What treasure do you have to offer?
Giving	How much would you need to give for it to qualify as sharing?
Growth	Take a step today toward storing up real treasure.

HOLY SMOKE! Read in Chapter 5 "Planned-Giving Basics," pages 75–78.

Insights   Questions

Day Twenty-Five
Leviticus 27:30-33
This ancient law describes the requirement for the Hebrew people to tithe as they
entered the Promised Land. Meditate on how this passage relates to you.

Grace	What makes something "holy to the Lord" (verse 30)?
Giftedness	Name ways in which sharing what you have is an expression of your giftedness.
Giving	Prayerfully consider the tithe (ten percent) as the benchmark for your financial giving.
Growth	Take a step today in moving from where you are in your giving to where you want to be.

Insights   Questions

Day Twenty-$ix
Deuteronomy 26:1-15

The passage describes the ritual for bringing the tithes into the sanctuary. It was an act of remembering on the part of the Hebrew people. Read the passage to discover the "why" of giving.

Grace	The Hebrews remembered God's saving acts on their behalf, including the Exodus. What do you have to remember for which you can give thanks?
Giftedness	The Hebrew people brought ten percent of their harvest. What do you have to bring?
Giving	How can your giving be an act of remembering God's acts of salvation on your behalf?
Growth	Take specific steps this week of moving toward giving as an act of remembering what God has done.

HOLY SMOKE! Read in Chapter 6 the introduction, "The Lord Owns Our Acquired Assets Too, Preacher!" and "Understanding the Second Pocket," pages 81–84.

Insights   Questions

Day Twenty-$even
Malachi 3:8-12

The prophet urges the Hebrew people to tithe, with the promise that if they do so, the whole nation will have plenty and live in the blessing of God. What would it be like if everyone had enough?

Grace	What would it be like if the "windows of heaven" (verse 10) were opened? Have you ever experienced this kind of blessing in your life?
Giftedness	Your giving is part of God's plan. Affirm the ways in which you participate in the work and will of God.
Giving	Consider the tithe (ten percent) as the benchmark for your financial giving.
Growth	Take a significant step toward this benchmark. If you tithe now, take a step beyond the benchmark of the tithe.

HOLY SMOKE! Read in Chapter 6 "Planning and Launching the Capital Campaign" and "A Concluding Word of Warning," pages 84–88.

Insights   Questions

Day Twenty-Eight
Matthew 23:23-24

Jesus advocates the discipline of tithing but warns against letting tithing become an object of applause from others. Have means, in a subtle way, become ends in your life?

Grace	What disciplines in your life have been a blessing for you?
Giftedness	What habits and disciplines can you affirm as wholesome in your life?
Giving	How can you keep your own financial giving from becoming an excuse for not undertaking specific actions of justice and mercy?
Growth	Prayerfully examine your motives for giving.

Insights   Questions

Day Twenty-Nine
Romans 12:3-8

There are a variety of gifts. Each person is promised at least one gift. We are called to use each gift we have received. Note that one of the gifts is generosity.

Grace	How have gifted individuals encouraged you in your faith journey?
Giftedness	Prayerfully search your own giftedness to see if your gifts match the list in Romans 12:3-8.
Giving	Is it possible that you might have the gift of generosity? If so, what would having this gift mean for your life?
Growth	Explore your giftedness throughout the day. Be open to recognizing and accepting a gift you might not have known you had.

Insights   Questions

Day Thirty
Luke 19:1-10

After an encounter with Jesus, Zacchaeus's life was radically changed. He had a new set of values. The new values were reflected in the way he managed his money. Does the way you allocate your money reflect the values you profess?

Grace	How has Jesus touched your life?
Giftedness	What abilities and assets do you have to share?
Giving	How will your spending and your giving reflect your values?
Growth	Make a step toward whatever benchmark you choose to set. We recommend the tithe as an initial benchmark to work toward and to move beyond.

Insights   Questions

Holy $moke!
Group Discussion of Chapters 5 and 6

Questions for discussion:
■ Are capital gifts and planned gifts a part of holy smoke?
■ Have you ever thought of tithing stocks or an estate?
■ Does your church have a planned-giving program?
■ What could your church do with a strong capital program?

Appendix II

Journeying Toward Whole-Life Stewardship: Readings for the Ten-Week Period

The Scripture readings that follow are to be used by members of the group journeying toward whole-life stewardship over a ten-week period. (See Chapter 4, pages 53–68, for an introduction and explanation of the process.)

There is only one Scripture passage assigned for each week; read the passage each day of the week. Keep a notebook handy as you read, and write down your reflections on the passage. Quite often the most helpful insights come only after reading the passage three, four, five, or six times. "Living with" a biblical passage for an entire week allows the Scripture and the reader to interact in a creative way.

After reading the passage of Scripture, use the questions below each week's reading to help you reflect on the themes of grace, giftedness, giving, and growth.

Week 1: Read 2 Corinthians 8.

Grace	What does the "generous act" of Jesus, in which he became poor for our sakes, say about the nature of God's grace (verse 9)?
Giftedness	How can you best use your gifts "first [for] the Lord" (verse 5)?
Giving	In this passage the Macedonian believers seem to combine giftedness and giving (generosity). How does generosity witness to Christ?
Growth	Verse 9 relates the giving of the Corinthians to the giving of Jesus. How does your giving relate to your faith in Jesus?

Week 2: Read Luke 4:16-19.

Grace	Think about the aspects of your life—food, clothing, shelter, hearing the good news. How have these gifts come to you?
Giftedness	What gifts do you have to help others receive food, clothing, shelter, and the good news of the gospel?
Giving	Can any of the gifts (food, clothing, shelter, the good news) happen through you without giving of your time and money?
Growth	What would be some benchmarks for your life around the above-mentioned items?

Week 3: Read Exodus 35 and 36.

Grace	Imagine having gifts beyond what you had dreamed possible. How would you use such gifts?
Giftedness	Are your gifts the kind that are noticed by others, or are they less visible in our society? Do you feel honored (by God) to have the gifts you have?
Giving	Imagine generous, overflowing giving. How does this make you feel?
Growth	How does a building help people grow? How does giving provide a witness?

Week 4: Read Matthew 25:31-46.

Grace	In what ways have you experienced grace through the kindness of others?
Giftedness	How can your giftedness be used to help "the least of these" (verse 40)?
Giving	What do you feel called to do for or with those who need what you are able to share?
Growth	Name areas in your life where you want to grow. Set benchmarks and timelines. Pray for God's grace as you take steps toward your benchmarks. Find a spiritual friend who will lovingly hold you accountable.

Week 5: Read Luke 18:9-14.

Grace	What is it like to receive a wonderful gift from an anonymous donor? Does it hinder your ability to enjoy the gift if there is no way to reciprocate?
Giftedness	Of the two persons in the story, who had the most to give? In what ways?
Giving	Make an anonymous gift this week that no one but the Lord sees you giving.
Growth	Remember when, as a small child, you wanted everyone to see all the tricks you had learned? Have you changed much since then? What steps can you take to grow in humility through giving?

Week 6: Read Ruth 1.

Grace	How has your family's love been a grace-filled (unearned) experience for you?
Giftedness	What specific gifts do you possess in your family? Name the gifts of others in the family.
Giving	What could you offer to a member of your family this week to enable that person's life to be more fulfilled?
Growth	What gift from a family member will do the most to enable your life to grow in the areas where you want and need to grow?

Week 7: Mark 10:13-16.

Grace	What does this story tell us about how God loves us and gives to us?
Giftedness	Children have gifts. How have the gifts of children been a blessing for you?
Giving	Do children receive gifts differently than adults? Has your attitude toward receiving changed since you were a child? Relate the answer to receiving the gift of God's kingdom.
Growth	Open yourself to noting and receiving God's blessings this week—even when you know you haven't earned them.

Week 8: Read Acts 4:32-37.

Grace	Imagine a group of Christians in which grace is so vividly experienced that everything they have would be shared.
Giftedness	What do you have to share with the fellowship of believers?
Giving	If a faith community like the one described in Acts 4 existed in your town (or within your congregation), how would you respond? Could you be a part of it?
Growth	What step does God want you to take this week to grow in your trust so that you will be able to share more fully?

Week 9: Read Ephesians 6:10-17.

Grace	Has God supplied you with all you need "to stand against the wiles of the devil" (verse 11)?
Giftedness	Name the strengths in your life that help you resist trials and temptations.
Giving	Share with someone this week out of the reservoir of your strength.
Growth	What benchmarks or disciplines will you set for your life? Write them down this week and develop a plan for working toward them.

Week 10: Read 2 Corinthians 9.

Grace	Joy experienced through giving is a gift from God; it is not a gift of our culture! The word for joy Paul uses in this passage could be translated "hilarity." Pray for the grace of generosity that brings joy to the inner self.
Giftedness	Paul talks about different people who used their gifts to accomplish certain things. What gifts do you have to use for good and for God?
Giving	What does 2 Corinthians 9 call you to do as next steps on your giving journey?
Growth	The Corinthian believers were to glorify God by the generosity of their sharing (verse 13). Set a benchmark for your giving that will glorify God.